Core Confidence

Stepping Into Your Greatest Potential-
Stepping Into Your Greatest Life

Cathy Patterson-Sterling MA, RCC

ISBN: 1-4781-0863-0
ISBN-13: 9781478108634

Contents

Acknowledgements

To God as my light and strength…
To my husband as my partner and best friend in life…
To my mother as my life time of support…
To my children for their love and sense of joy…
To my girlfriends who show me laughter every day…
To my clients for allowing me to be your scribe over the years…
To my team who help bring God's plans into a workable reality!

Introduction: When We Lose Ourselves Along The Way

For Anyone Who Has Lost Themselves Along The Way…

Have you ever looked into the mirror and not liked what you were seeing back in the reflection? At some point in life, individuals may even feel like they have become a shell of who it is they used to be as they feel lost inside. Many people are battling a wave of discontentment or even insecurity that is percolating underneath the surface of their lives. Such people are doing all they can just to keep themselves above the wave without going under. These individuals feel lost like they are filling their lives up with stuff. They are busy, but they are also riding an emotional rollercoaster of highs and lows with worry or at the other extreme they are emotionally flat-lining through life whereby they feel disconnected or shut-down. Such people have lost themselves along the way.

When we feel lost at different points in time, our emotional worlds become smaller. We may be preoccupied with just trying to manage the busyness of each day of our lives or our emotional worlds may become focused on others as we worry a lot about what other people think of us because we have become people-pleasers. We may even start losing our self-esteems as we begin living for the approval of others. Essentially, we feel lost. Some people are lost in what their spouses are doing or not doing especially if there are lies, deceptions, or secret behaviours in the household like hidden pornography problems, acting-out with spending of money, and so on. Individuals may feel lost in working crazy long hours trying to pay for a lifestyle that comes with a heavy financial price tag as well as emotional cost. Meanwhile some people are lost in reacting like an emotional yo-yo rebounding off situations around what other individuals are doing or not doing. Then there are others who feel lost because they have dreams but do not feel like they have the time, resources, or even the confidence to go after them.

These percolating emotional undercurrents underneath the surface come and go in waves. At times we may feel like we are managing okay only to have that yucky feeling take over again like a giant wave that is going to sweep us up and pound us into the sand. We have a sensation of slipping on an emotional level. As we go out into the world we may look wonderful and all "put together" nicely while attending church or meeting with others. In our jobs, people may depend on us to know what is going on and we may even be leaders. The reality, however, is that inside many of us there is a wave that surfaces in our thoughts during those still moments in time when looking in the mirror or laying our heads down on our pillows before sleeping. Not all is right in our emotional worlds and to some degree we feel lost.

How I Lost Myself Along The Way

I came to the Lord when I was a young teenager. My world opened up and I had an amazing connection to God. I had found a friend, peace within myself, and I could feel God's hand of grace pour over me. At a deeper level, I knew I was not alone in this world. The Lord infused me with such grace that I could feel my soul filling up from the inside out overflowing with His love. The difficulty was that my understanding of my relationship with God was an immature one. I thought God was my personal genie. At the age of 14, I remember sitting on a cliff overlooking Blue Lake praying to God: "When I get older I want to marry Marty Sterling. And by the way can you make that happen when I am 21 because that works for me." Due to an unfortunate sequence of events in one of my outings with Mr. Sterling (when he was at the ripe age of 18), in his great wisdom he decided to take me out for a hike and shot a squirrel. I declared him a savage beast and refused to talk to him for seven years! After those years, I would vaguely communicate a greeting to him with a tone of major aloofness. Then one day he called me and I gave him a second chance so long as no shooting of rodents was involved. We dated and were married a year later. We began building a life together. I was not 21. Instead, I was 29 when we married.

I had the ideal dream in my mind of a large house, three children (my order into God was two girls and a boy), and I wanted a career. Not just a little job but a full blown six figure, top boss career. I wanted it all...the house, the kids, the senior executive career, and the love of my life. I was so focused on my goals and getting what I wanted in life that I put my health needs on the backburner. Back in my early twenties, I had developed a genetic form of arthritis and managed it with medication as well as with an active lifestyle. During my pregnancies, I had to go off my medication and my mobility became more compromised. I didn't care. I wanted to build my outside life at all costs! As I poured myself into building my world, God became very distant from my thinking and my life. Who needed God when you have goals and a hard work ethic? My thinking was that you just build your world and make it happen. The reality was that I was a control-freak at the driver's wheel of my life. I didn't realize that I was about to drive over an emotional cliff.

Then in one instant it all started to crash around me! All that I had worked for was about to disintegrate. I had worn my health down to the point where I had not only had extreme levels of sleep apnea (I never bothered to notice I wasn't sleeping for 10 years and was choking myself awake 75 times an hour), I had fused both of my knees with my arthritis and I was preparing for life in a wheelchair. Still, I didn't care. I had things to do, children to raise, and a life to build according to my expectations. Along the way I became completely lost when all the while I thought I was just focused and was a hard worker.

Then one day, all that I had worked for in my career was about to be destroyed in an instant. One of my colleagues had broken trust to such a degree that my professional reputation by association was about to be tarnished. More importantly, the wonderful income I thought that I needed to fuel my life was about to be snuffed out as the business around me was on the verge of financial collapse. I broke. I fell to my knees and I cried as I was inconsolable. My world was crashing around me. In my mind, I was about to lose everything. I was going to be in a wheelchair, my career was over, and the great lifestyle I had built along with my family was about to be popped like a balloon in an instant.

Before a class I was teaching, I sat with a dear friend when the wave of tears came pouring out. He looked at me and said: "Cathy you are being a powerboat powering your way through life on self-will. Aren't you burning out? You don't have to be that powerboat and instead you can be a sail boat if you put God back at the center of your life. The Lord is your wind and with His will you will charter a course beyond your dreams." My friend Peter who used to be a student of mine years ago and who now had more wisdom than all of my years put together talked about the yoke of God and how His burden is light (Mathew 11:30).

An easier life with God at the center of it? Seriously?

That was beyond my comprehension but I was so broken and I had lost myself along the way. I was out of control and I was grasping at the shattered pieces trying to assemble them back together into some constructive form that resembled my life.

I had no choice but to rebuild myself from the inside out. No one could fill up the emptiness in me. My husband loved me and my children were and still are amazing. But that sliding feeling of panic, being out of control, lost, and insecure on the deepest levels possible was all in me. My outer world, no matter how big I built it could not mask the innermost parts of me that lurked in the shadows of insecurity. Yes, I could build a great life or even an envious one but inside I still had to contend with me.

So I began the journey of bringing God back into the center of my life again. I wasn't sure how that all worked. I didn't think He even wanted me. I had abandoned Him and I was such a control-freak how was I even supposed to hand my life to Him? What if I had pain? What if situations did not work out? You mean I had to give up control? Seriously?

I started talking to God and I read through the bible from beginning to end. Also, I read Dallas Willard's *The Spirit of The Disciplines* and John Eldredge's *Walking With God* and I started the walk. I invited God into everything in my life....every decision, every thought and I kept conscious contact with God throughout much of each day.

In fact, I began a process of peeling back the layers and handing myself in complete vulnerability to God. I could feel His love and His tempering and refining of me. The Lord wanted to mold me and I was forced to die unto old parts of myself. I learned about giving up control and most importantly I learned about surrendering my will. Over time, I sat in prayer with God and really opened my ears to listen for when He said "No", "Not now," or "Not this way." For a control-freak like me, the word no is not a pleasant word. I was the gas in life and I needed God to not only serve as my brakes but also to be the driver of my bus. Furthermore, I needed to live in His will for not only my personal freedom but for my sanity. I was tired of driving over emotional cliffs and powering my way through life.

Then one day a strange set of events occurred. I met someone who had the same arthritis as me and their disease was arrested and stopped in it's tracks. This lead to a journey to Mexico where I met a Rheumatologist who provided me with the medication I needed to stop the arthritis and the pain. This journey involved me travelling down to one of the most dangerous border crossings in the world and navigating through border patrol police crashing around me in sand dunes while they looked for migrant workers illegally going across the unmanned areas of the border. Through a strange set of events I travelled alone and on God's will. I was scared, I had a massive meltdown alone in a dated, makeshift x-ray lab in Mexico with a poor attendant who could not speak English all the while trusting God and where He was leading me on this journey. Out of that series of events, I realized I was eligible for knee replacement surgery and I had the operation completed back in Canada.

After the surgery, I had to learn how to walk again and rebuild my core strength. With extensive physiotherapy I was much like a new baby in my 40's walking out into the world.

Learning to walk again was a challenge. My heels had not touched the ground for 10 years of my life. I was embarrassed, prideful, and had to be vulnerable as I followed the instructions from my Physiotherapist around how to learn to walk again. All the while, I kept inviting God into my life through conversation as well as prayer and I trusted Him.

In this journey I learned about rebuilding my core body strength and most importantly about rebuilding my emotional core with God at the center of my life. I am a Clinical Counsellor. Over this period of time in life, I continued counselling my clients and as I started to get myself back from the inside out, I realized that many of clients were on a similar journey of losing themselves somewhere along the way. They had addicted family members, husbands with pornography problems, were on a massive self-esteem spiral because their spouses had affairs, and so on. Many of these people were lost and were learning to "walk again." The worlds they had built for themselves were shattered in an instant through broken trust and always in situations they had never anticipated. So many of my clients have said to me "This is not what I signed up for" as they recalled the breaking down of their marriages while we walked through the process of rebuilding. More important than questions of whether people would get back together or not in their marriages was the question of whether my clients would reclaim their lives and get themselves back? They were lost, they were mad at God, and similarly they had to go through a process of being vulnerable by peeling back the layers. They had parts of themselves they had to die unto which with a mountain of pride was extremely difficult when with every fibre of their being they wanted to point their fingers at their husbands and say: "I am this way because HE DID THIS!!!!" The rage and overwhelming insecurity they felt was consuming them.

Similarly, I met with clients who had lost themselves along the way as they built "outside worlds" for themselves and focused on their careers only to find themselves at the top of their empires with a bottle of alcohol in their hands to drown away the overwhelming stress they experienced while keeping these empires afloat. Where was God in the mixture? It didn't matter for them because their God had become the bottle.

This is a book for anyone who has lost themselves along the way. Such people may have put all of their energies into building an outside world for themselves by focusing on their marriages and families or even their careers. In our society, most of us want it all and we go to work building a life for ourselves. Self-will can serve as the necessary power engine that we need to accomplish our goals. But at the end of the day when we look in the mirror we are still stuck with ourselves. When that sliding feeling surfaces within ourselves, that edge of insecurity, that inner feeling of being out of control, a deep abyss of emptiness, or whatever sensation we experience it is an indication that something is wrong. No outside thing like the house, car, career, goals, new school for our children, and so forth will fill us up. The challenge is to build ourselves from the inside out and to strengthen our emotional core so that we gain emotional resiliency and are ready for anything. This ability is what we will refer to as *emotional fitness*. With emotional fitness, we become resilient and can "power up" to deal with challenges. Most importantly when we grow with God at the center of our lives that percolating edge of emptiness or panic inside dissolves. We find a freedom as we give up control in our worlds and walk with God. Furthermore, we become equipped for anything and with a strong sense of core confidence we step into God's larger story and plans for our lives.

Chapter 1
The Erosion Of Confidence

What is confidence? Essentially, confidence is the belief in one's self and one's powers or abilities. When we walk out a sense of confidence we are able to "power up" and have the strength to do anything. We know we can do it as we charter a course and get the job done with focus as well as determination. So there is confidence in accomplishing our goals, but there is also personal confidence which means standing solid in who we are. We do not give others the power to "knock us off balance" or make us second-guess ourselves. Instead, we stand strong with strength knowing for ourselves that what we are thinking or what we decide on doing is right for us.

Did we even have confidence and did we lose our confidence somewhere along the way? The answer depends on the story of your life. Some people had that strong sense of confidence and now they feel like a shell of who they used to be. Such individuals feel lost inside likely because of responding to years of stress in their personal or even professional lives that has slowly eroded away at their self-esteems. Then there are other people who have lived much of their lives with a legacy of insecurity in that they are overly-concerned with the thoughts as well as judgments of others. Such individuals are people-pleasers and they guess in advance what will "please" others as they shut down their thoughts as well as feelings in order to accommodate other people. People-pleasers may have not had a chance to grow into their confidence because they have held themselves back since they are worried about how they are viewed in the eyes of the people around them. Such individuals have conformed themselves to their own small emotional boxes as they live according to the anticipated wrath or judgment of what other people think of them.

The challenge is to grow into a sense of *core confidence* which means building ourselves from the inside out that is independent of other people's opinions or judgments. With core confidence we develop a voice, we honor our feelings, we have a personal truth, and we raise our value. With such a tool box of skills of *emotional fitness* we are prepared as we have the confidence to step into the greater potential of our lives.

Why We Lose Ourselves

The reason we lose our confidence is because we attach to something external outside of ourselves. Our sense of personal value or "being okay" is connected to something directly outside of ourselves which may include our need for validation from others so we feel okay if others think we are okay as we gain their approval. Another external is when we attach our personal value to outside success indicators. For example, we feel okay when we look okay or the world is reflecting back to us that we are okay. Success indicators may be the nice clothes we wear, the fancy car, a high powered career, a perfect weight goal, an immaculate house and so on. The path to insecurity and feeling out of control is rooted in attaching ourselves to something outside of ourselves. We then begin to ride an emotional rollercoaster of highs and lows because we have secured our entire self-worth and how we feel about ourselves to something outside of our inner emotional core. This means that we can only be okay so long is everything in our outer world is okay. When there are problems or crisis, if we do not have a strong emotional core (a sense of being okay inside no matter what) then we will feel like our lives are falling apart. We will not be able to handle the stress.

Losing Ourselves In People-Pleasing
"If You Think I Am Okay Then I Am Okay"

One of the reasons we attach to what people say or do and go down into a spiral or destabilize (feel like we are "losing it"), is because we have patterns of people-pleasing. Out of our needs to be accepted we place ourselves on the end of other people's emotional yo-yo's and we take a backseat in life to other people's feelings. In other words, we bounce off of what other people say and do around us much like a yo-yo. We worry about their approval and if we look okay in "their eyes." If we feel that we are not getting that approval or validation then we panic inside. Furthermore, we shut down parts of who we are and deny what we think or feel in order to gain the approval of others. How we are seen in the eyes of other people is most important to us. Some of us may even hand over our sense of self-esteems or personal self-worth to others for their evaluation. If they do not think we are okay, then we must not be okay as people is the underlying belief.

Managing Situations

People-pleasing is an exhausting way of coping in life. In order to be a successful people-pleaser you need to anticipate the approval or disapproval of what others will think in any given situation. Such action involves making assumptions around what other people are thinking. For example, as people-pleasers we become good at reading other individuals' body language or we place ourselves "in the shoes of others" as we guess around what they will like, dislike, or think at any given moment. Then in order to avoid that anticipated disapproval from others, people-pleasers have to manage a situation and change their own behaviour in order to make it okay for others so that they can gain approval. Therefore people-pleasers have to take the time to get to know the likes and dislikes or opinions of others, shift situations part way through to make sure everything looks okay or that they are "doing the right thing" in the eyes of others, and then hopefully gain the approval they are craving so that they can feel okay about themselves as well as their worlds for a moment.

A People-Pleaser In Action:

Ann wants to celebrate her job promotion with her boyfriend Jake. He has worked hard all week and is a bit of a "homebody" in that he likes to stay at home and watch movies or a lot of television during his "down-time" from work. She knows he will not want to go out for dinner but she wants to do something to celebrate. Ann thinks about how Jake will likely just want to sit on the couch and fall asleep part way through watching TV. Rather than risk the disapproval from Jake, Ann begins a process of talking herself out of her feelings. She says to herself: "Well maybe it isn't such a big deal that I got that promotion and raise. I don't really want to bother Jake since he has had a long week working out of town. He needs his rest. I don't want to bug him so I'll just tuck in beside him on the couch and not really make a big deal out of this promotion thing anyways!"

As a people-pleaser Ann has effectively managed this situation by anticipating Jake's reaction, talking herself out of her feelings, emotionally shutting-down part of herself, and conforming to laying on a couch on Friday night because she does not want to be a "bother" to Jake.

People-pleasers also exhaust themselves because they are masters at pretending that everything is okay when it is not. Such individuals nod in agreement when someone they care about is saying something even when inside they are screaming in disagreement yet they say nothing. In fact, people-pleasers are masters at not "making waves" or "rocking the boat" so that they can gain the approval of others.

Let's flash back to the example with Ann and Jake. On Friday night Jake comes home after working a long week and he is not tired. He says to Ann (who has not seen him all week): "Ann, I know you just wanted to stay home and have a quiet night anyways, but I am wondering if you mind if I go and visit some buddies of mine tonight. They are having a game of poker and getting some guys together that I haven't seen in a long time." With every fibre of her being, Ann wants to say no and mention her job promotion as well as the plans she had hoped for with going out for dinner. But as a people-pleaser, Ann does not want to upset Jake so she pretends that everything is fine as she quietly says: "Sure." Now on Friday evening Ann sits on the couch alone cuddled up by herself crying because a happy moment like a job promotion which is wonderful became an "ugly moment" in two seconds not even worth celebrating since she is alone at home by herself.

Another exhausting feature of the people-pleasing pattern is that if people-pleasers suspect that others do not think highly of them or are disapproving of something they have said or done then they feel crushed inside. People-pleasers will let the perceived disapproval of others "rent space" in their minds or thoughts for a long time. Such people will "beat themselves up" going over in their thoughts what they should have said or done differently in order to gain that approval from others at the end of the day.

In the example with Ann and Jake let's have this situation take another turn. When Jake asks Ann if it bothers her that he is going out with his friends Ann may say: "Actually, I kind of wanted to stay home with you tonight. I haven't seen you all week!" Ann scans for Jake's reaction and sees that he has stepped back and has a snarl on his face. She can sense the disapproval. Ann panics inside. Jake says: "Now you are mad aren't you?" Ann says: "No. Go ahead." Jake says: "Well if you don't want me to go then say so now and I won't go!" Ann says: "Nope, it's fine. Just go." Now this situation "rents space" in Ann's mind because she is worried that Jake thinks she is mad at him. Her time on the couch alone that evening is a restless one.

The Emotional Rollercoaster

People-pleasers place their personal value on other people's views of them. Essentially, people-pleasers are handing their personal power over to others. This is a recipe for instability and an emotional rollercoaster because we can never be comfortable in other people's perceptions which are always changing. Also, we may anticipate what others are thinking and then torment ourselves because we feel like we are not meeting those grand expectations that we do not even know are true or correct in the first place.

With a people-pleasing cycle an emotional rollercoaster is in effect because people-pleasers have a sense of "being okay" momentarily and only if they are getting feedback from people that they are "doing well", making the right decisions, or are receiving praise. If people-pleasers sense emotional withdrawal, rejection, emotional distance, or some other negative reaction then they will experience extreme emotional lows. Therefore people-pleasers are constantly riding a cycle of highs and lows (like a rollercoaster) as they match-up or synchronize with others to try and gain active approval.

Casting Shadows Of Disapproval

Many people-pleasers live in an emotional trap or box because they have lost their self-esteems in whether they gain approval or not from others. If such people- pleasing people make decisions that are not approved by others then there is a metaphorical shadow cast over them so that if they make a mistake or things do not work out as planned then other disapproving individuals will say "We told you so!" This is a people-pleaser's greatest nightmare that if they step out of the approval of others then they are left on their own to fail. Not only do they have to suffer the humiliation of defeat, but they also have the added emotional injury of other people's disapproval and being made to feel bad because of these perceived failures.

When we have a people-pleasing pattern going on in our lives we cannot step into a sense of strong core confidence.

The Effects Of People-Pleasing:

-We give our power away and second-guess ourselves based on what others say to us about our own potential as well as abilities.

-We please others at the expense of ourselves and struggle with saying no or setting limits.

-We allow other people's criticisms get to us.

-We worry about other people's approval of us and how we "look in their eyes."

-We feel guilty or responsible for other people's feelings.

-We allow others to blame us for their problems and we take on their feelings instead of letting them deal with their own issues to some degree.

-We feel like we are a victim to other people's actions. They are "doing things to us" to make us feel bad instead of us taking responsibility for our own feelings/actions.

-We are often upset with others and have problems communicating this frustration with them.

-We are often resentful of others and do not resolve these issues. Instead, we talk ourselves out of our feelings and convince ourselves that what we are feeling or seeing is not real. Instead, we second-guess ourselves and give others the "constant benefit of the doubt."

-We worry that others close to us are going to reject or abandon us.

-When others are angry, emotionally-withdraw, or shut-down we worry about what we have done and take on their issues trying to make peace because we have fears of conflict.

-We do not get over issues with people or "rebound" back quickly.

-We become overwhelmed easily.

Guilt- The Unwelcome Houseguest That Never Leaves

When we are trapped in a people-pleasing cycle in our lives we live with guilt. Essentially guilt is the feeling of responsibility or remorse for committing a wrong. The problem with people-pleasing, however, is that we constantly feel like we are doing things in a wrong way. As people-pleasers, we live for the approval of others and when we do not gain that approval or affirmation then we feel like we have done something wrong. We are easily manipulated into feeling bad or guilty when we have not pleased others. A huge difficulty is that the people we are trying to "please" may be unreasonable in that they are trying to control or manipulate us into doing what it is that they want. Therefore such people "activate our guilt buttons" and as people-pleasers we feel bad as we back down to do whatever it is that will make those individuals happy even if it comes at the expense of ourselves.

For example:

Sara joined a meeting at church to find out in a random way, almost by accident, by reading the meeting notes from last time that someone had signed her up to lead the worship team's project with introducing new technology to an updated music program. She was in charge of purchasing the equipment, assembling the new music arrangements, and the list went on and on. In total this could be as long as a six month full time project. Sara asked why she had been assigned to this huge responsibility? Of course she had not told anyone yet that her and her husband were expecting their first child.

Someone in the group mentioned that she was "super organized" and "was good at music" so rather than nominating her for the project, they went ahead and signed her up. Sara was fuming in anger, but she began talking herself out of her feelings. She was upset that no one had the respect to even talk to her about this project and that there was an assumption that she would go ahead and do it. Sara said: "So everyone assumed I would just do this?" One of the members said: "Well you are the best that we have and without you this new program will not take off. Also the congregation needs some updated arrangements and with the new technology we may get people more engaged in the services. Without you that may take forever and may not happen." Rather than saying: "Why is it all on me to make this happen?", Sara began feeling guilty even though she was pregnant and needed to slow down her pace in life. Sara started to focus on the disappointment of others and how they needed the expanded music ensembles with the added technology. As Sara thought more about it, perhaps she could work really hard in the upfront, beginning part of her pregnancy to get this work over with and then slow down later?

The root of guilt is the feeling "I need to do what it is you want me to do or I am not okay in your eyes." People-pleasers live with an incredible fear of disappointing others. In the above example, Sara compromised the health of herself and her baby with an extreme work schedule in order to not "disappoint" others.

Guilt is like an unwanted houseguest that never leaves as it sets up residence within us. Furthermore, with guilt we have eroded self-esteems. We begin a process of shutting ourselves down in order to gain other people's approval. Furthermore, we deny our value, our truth, our feelings, or even our reality. Instead, we talk ourselves into what other people want for us in order to gain their approval. We have then placed ourselves on the end of other people's emotional yo-yo's and when we try to pull back or stand in our value or truth we are jerked back into place out of the leverage of guilt. Either we feel bad for not pleasing that other person or we live in fear that we will not have their approval and that they will somehow think badly of us.

In an intellectual way this is fascinating that the houseguest of guilt is making the owner of the house feel bad when guilt has nothing to offer but bad will and yucky feelings. Guilt is a useless emotion when we feel bad around something we should not feel terrible about and with guilt we allow others to leverage control over our lives. Often as people-pleasers, we destabilize and do what we can to get back the approval of others.

Pack Your Bags We Are Going On A Guilt Trip!

People around us are more than prepared to make us feel bad or "guilty" as they "dish out guilt" so that we will do what they want at any time.

For example:

-You are asked to do something.

-You explain why you cannot fulfill that request.

-Then the person says to you: “Oh r______e______a______ l______l______y ?”

-The word “really” becomes 10 syllables and is drawn out with a hook. This is the guilt signal of disapproval.

-A people-pleaser will accept this hook, back-down, and then do what the other person is requesting out of fear of disapproval. The ridiculous nature of the request often does not matter and people-pleasers (in order to avoid guilt and fear of disappointing others) will talk themselves out of their feelings and resentfully do what is requested of them even if it comes as a cost to themselves in terms of their time, inconvenience, health, finances, and so on.

The Guilt Bombs People Are Prepared To Toss Our Way

Guilt Bomb #1:

People will accuse us of not “supporting them” if we do not do what they want us to.

A common statement:

“Of all the people, I thought I could count on you for your help and support!”

People-pleasers feel bad, wrong, or inadequate for not “supporting” or doing what other people want them to.

Guilt Bomb #2:

People will get mad and use emotional withdrawal as well as one word answers until we do what they want.

Common statements:

“Whatever”, “Yes”, “No.”

People-pleasers will sense the emotional withdrawal and distancing from another person who provides one word answers to responses. Of course people-pleasers want to “make it right” by trying to get back the affection so they work hard to please the other person and make them stop being mad.

Guilt Bomb #3:

Emotional hostage-taking occurs when people ask us to do something and if we say "no" then we know that we will receive an emotional punishment of some kind in that they will not talk to us for a period of time or they will act cold as well as unaffectionate.

A common statement:

"Fine do whatever you want!" (Then the emotional withdrawal and punishment of silence occurs).

People-pleasers accept this subtle punishment and do what the person wants even though they do not want to because they have fears of the emotional withdrawal which feels like rejection or even abandonment to them.

People-Pleasing In Motion- A Climate Of Emotional Eggshells

When we have people-pleasing patterns in our lives, we can easily participate in "emotional hostage-taking situations" in our relationships. This means that people-pleasing can go to such a level that individuals feel like they are "walking on eggshells" out of fear of saying or doing the wrong thing that will upset others. These people-pleasers become "emotional hostages" doing things not within their will because they have a fear of rejection, disapproval, or worry of disappointing others.

When we hand our power over to others by worrying so much about their reactions that we compromise ourselves in order to "please" those individuals regardless of the cost to ourselves, then we begin to erode our personal confidence as well as self-esteems. We have effectively placed metaphorical eggshells around ourselves and are so fearful of upsetting another person that we end up "walking on eggshells" careful not to create an emotional disturbance. Over time, we attune ourselves to "pleasing" others at all costs and we adjust our actions to whether this would be approving to them or not. The larger problem is that we can end up losing ourselves in other people's approval and we reward bad behaviour on their side. If we pretend everything is okay when it is not, we shut down parts of who we are, talk ourselves out of our feelings, and do whatever is necessary to keep others happy regardless of how we feel inside, then we are engaging in the active care as well as feeding of emotional bullies. Bullies know they can leverage power over others in order to get what they want. Emotional bullies will erode our confidence each and every time.

Characteristics Of An Eggshell Dance:

- I worry that if I say or do the wrong thing then the other person will get mad, emotionally withdraw, not talk to me, or isolate. I interpret this as a punishment and work hard not to "set them off."

-I anticipate what they will do and then try to make everything better so that they are not upset.

-I end up rewarding bad behaviour in others because I never let them know they have hurt my feelings or have reached a limit. Instead, I accept their poor treatment and work hard to please them. As a result I open myself up to being controlled as well as manipulated because I have fears of conflict as well as rejection.

-There is no honesty as I deny what I think and feel in order to please someone else.

Why We Allow Ourselves To Walk On Eggshells

As people-pleasers we live with a worry around disappointing others because we have a fear of abandonment as well as rejection. When others emotionally withdraw, as people-pleasers we panic and sense their distancing. As a result, we work hard to "make things right" or get that attention as well as affection back. The problem is that we are being controlled and others will pull their affection away so that we do what it is they want. These people do more controlling than they do communicating. If we are people-pleasers, then our self-esteems are eroded because of our fears of abandonment which takes over our relationships.

Often people-pleasers have fears of conflict as they are frequently overwhelmed as well as exhausted by the willful behaviour of other individuals. People-pleasers may feel like they have to "match wills" or engage in a debate they know they will not win in order to express themselves. For people-pleasers it is often easier just to "dive under the wave" and "follow the line of least resistance" by giving in and not arguing back a particular point. It is just easier to "duck under the wave of intensity" of another person.

Giving Our Power Away

When we are bothered when others pull away their approval or withdraw their affection because we are not doing what they want, then we end up in a pattern or a dance whereby we keep giving our power away. This means that we are open and available for others to emotionally dismiss us as we allow people to "knock us off balance" on an emotional level.

Emotional dismissal occurs when other people tell us what we think or feel is wrong. For example, in the earlier example with Jake and Ann. Jake does not return until the next evening after going out with his friends. He makes an excuse around how he was having fun and forgot to call. Ann is angry that he is treating her with such disrespect. She explains how she is upset that he did not have the respect to call her and was away all weekend especially when she did not see him all week. Jake says: "Ann, you are being ridiculous. I was just enjoying time with my friends. It's not a big deal." Ann continues to explain how she would have appreciated a call at the very least to know that something bad did not happen to him. Jake says: "Ann, I know I could have called. But really I think you are over-reacting." In this situation, Jake is dismissing Ann's feelings. Ann senses Jake's frustration and rather than resolving this issue she begins "walking on eggshells" careful to not "push this issue too far" and upset him. She is careful to "bury this issue" and not bring it up again.

When we allow ourselves to be people-pleasers then we erode our confidence in our personal relationships and this impacts our self-esteems. As people-pleasers, we end up shutting down parts of how we feel by denying our feelings as well as accepting poor treatment from others. The difficulty also is that we stop setting limits in our relationships and we allow other individuals to leverage power over us. Rather than setting boundaries around people's disrespectful behaviour, as people-pleasers we look at how we can gain emotional approval or affection from others. If we have a conflict, then we think we have done something wrong and work hard to make things better from our side. The difficulty is that we give our power away and open ourselves up to not only "walking on emotional eggshells" but we also tolerate emotional bullying from others who are prepared to launch "guilt bombs", make us feel bad about ourselves, or leverage power as a way to get us to do what it is that they want.

Emotional bullies are not necessarily bad people and they may have a lot of wonderful qualities as well as characteristics, but they are prepared to use guilt or even a force of will to get whatever it is that they want. In fact, emotional bullies will often "bulldoze" or take advantage of others with people-pleasing patterns in life.

The Modus Operandi Of Emotional Bullies

-Things must be "my way" and I will do all that I can to ensure it goes my way despite the emotional cost to others.

-If other people do not help me "get my way" then there will be a punishment, emotional fall-out or a cost to them and I will make sure they regret not helping me get my way. For example, I will punish them by name-calling, not talking to them, emotional cut-off, withdrawal of finances, and so on. I will make it miserable for them until they relent and give me what I want.

-Emotional hostage-taking. For example: "You better do what I want or else…"

-I will match you in will and I will overpower you at all costs until I get my way. I do not care what it takes so long as I win in the end and get what I want.

-I zone in on what I want and will "steam roll over you" if necessary.

-I will "out-argue" you and make you feel stupid until you give in and help me get what I want.

-I will sulk as well as pout until I get what I want.

-I do not care whether you are feeling weak, vulnerable, or are upset. Actually I see this as an opportunity to capitalize on your weakness and force the issue of getting what I want. When you are weak, I position myself as strong.

-I will send all kinds of guilt signals around your worth and value to manipulate you until I get what I want. When you feel bad and "back-off" then I will rush in and get what I want. I will praise you then for doing what it is that I want.

-I will hold power or influence over you and remind you of how I call the shots and will tell you what it is that I want you to do.

-I will make you feel scared as well as unsafe because my behaviours are all over the place and I am volatile. You never know when I am going to get upset.

-I will relentlessly badger you and wear you down until I get what I want. In my world no means wear you down until you say yes.

-I will recruit other people into feeling sorry for me and with their help I will make you look bad if you get in my way. I will tell you what "others" are saying about you as a way to manipulate you and make you feel bad.

Examples Of Different Types Of Bullies

Intellectual Bully: "Don't try and stand up to me. I will make you look stupid and out-argue you if you try. In, fact I can run circles around you in any argument."

Financial Bully: "I hold the money and the power. You cannot make decisions unless I give you permission and release the funds that come with it."

Emotional Bully: "Do what I want or you will regret it. I will make you pay no matter how long it takes. You won't try that again"

Shame Bully: "Here is another example of the silly little mistakes you make all the time! I swear if I didn't have to think for you, I don't know what you would do."

Arrogant Bully: "I made you who you are. You would be nothing without me."

The Greatest Tactics For Emotional Bullies

Bullies gain ground in a power differential. If you stand up to them, then they will try to leverage power over you. For example their attitude is much like saying: "Look at what I will do to you, if you do that." Furthermore, bullies have the ability to know the secret fears of others and they will activate these fears by "playing mind games" around these fears in order to have more power, control, as well as influence. In fact, bullies will play on people's fears in order to get what they want.

One of the most powerful techniques that bullies use is to "play mind games" around giving attention or compliments and then withdrawing affection or attention in accordance with whether you are doing what they want or not. Furthermore, bullies are "master debaters" who try to out-argue, intellectualize, or dominate conversations in order to gain control as well as influence. In most situations, bullies will "bulldoze" or dominate over the needs of others. Such bullies always "want their own way" and on their own terms.

Bullies grow stronger when others provide "victim signals" or show signs of weakness. As you are weaker, bullies grow stronger as well as braver in strength. If you reward bad behaviour by giving in, taking on the blame, and apologizing when an individual is bullying, then this pattern continues. The person has a "pay-off" or advantage for bullying.

Of course bullies love to shame others and make them feel insecure as well as inadequate. They gain strength because people-pleasers will often second-guess themselves as it may feel easier to just give the bully what he/she wants or believe you are "the crazy person" then deal with the exhausting levels of conflict that bullies can bring to situations.

Bullies love to use "you made me feel" statements as they try to "guilt you out" around not doing what they want. Guilt and shame are a bully's favourite tactics. For example a bully will say: "I thought you would have....(*guilt*), but you didn't....and that is because you are...(*shame*)."

The Line of Least Resistance

Many people give in to emotional bullying because it is easier to just "duck" under the wave of intensity as well as conflict coming at you and to give in then to deal with the exhausting levels of drama if the bully does not get what they want. Some people think if they just give emotional bullies what they want, then at least they will be left alone in peace for a while. What they do not realize is that they are rewarding or reinforcing the bad behaviour of bullies. By "giving in" every time, bullies learn that the word "no" does not apply to them and that they just need to leverage power, make others feel guilty, or wear others down until they get what they want.

Losing Ourselves In Managing Others
"If I Make You Okay, Then I Will Be Okay"

Many people get lost along the way because they are trying to "manage someone else's unhealthiness." For example, individuals may have spouses who are "acting-out" and struggling with addiction or issues of some kind. Such people may be trying very hard to deal with self-destructive or even dishonest behaviours of their "acting-out spouses" especially when these acting-out behaviours appear to stabilize and then surface again suddenly out of nowhere. For example, a wife may think that her husband's pornography problem is under control only to find out that these behaviours have merely gone "off the radar", are "underground" or are just hidden from sight from everyone for a while. Such spouses feel "emotionally blindsided" as they detect the lies as well as deceit again from their "acting-out" partners. Then these spouses are on guard waiting for another moment of chaos or series of upsetting events. Little do these people know that they are slowly getting sucked into a pattern of trying to manage someone else who has behaviour that is completely out of control.

The "Chasing Down The Truth" Game

One way that people try to "manage" the lives of others is they run around trying to sort out all the lies, half-truths, or omission of details from others who are "acting-out" with deceitful or addictive behaviours. Such people waste an enormous amount of life energy trying to detect the truth, find out information, and make their way through the lies. This is an exhausting way of living as people end up taking on roles of becoming emotional spies or detectives over their own spouses who are "acting-out." Much of the life energy people waste is on "chasing down the truth" or sorting out the reality of how they are being lied to on so many occasions.

For example:

Kelly knows that her husband John has a sex addiction and that he has built a "secret life" whereby he does "sexting" and talks to women on the internet about sexual fantasies. John says he "has stopped all that stuff." Kelly knows better and she is constantly looking for opportunities to "catch him in his lies" by grabbing his cell phone when he is not looking to see what he has been up to lately and if he has "left a trail of evidence" or she waits until he goes outside to the garage to quickly do a scan of his computer. Kelly is trying to "manage the truth" and she has become an expert manager of John's life.

Rescuing

Another way people try to "manage" the lives of others is that they think they can "bring out the good side" of others who are "acting-out." People with rescuing patterns will try to save, help, or make things better for others who are in a constant state of chaos.

For example:

Shelly knows her son has a drinking problem and he is always spending money. She constantly worries about him and she is looking for ways to make things better so that he won't be discouraged. This month he cannot come up with his rent money because he has spent it all partying. Shelly "rescues" him from this situation by paying for his rent and loading up his fridge with groceries.

With the "chasing down the truth" and rescuing patterns, people become expert managers of other individual's lives. Such people are trying to manage the "unhealthiness" of others and often believe at a deeper level if they can "make others okay first" then they "themselves will be okay." What such people do not realize is that they are getting lost in managing the unhealthiness of others. These individuals will continue to lose themselves in the unmanageability of other people's lives as they experience chronic stress, fatigue, exhaustion, and emotional burn-out. The challenge is to love other people who are struggling, but to "unhook" and allow these individuals with unhealthy patterns to take responsibility for their own lives. If we try to make everyone else around us "okay" while ignoring our own health, needs, feelings, or reality then we will start to lose our identities as well as self-esteems in the dysfunction and unhealthy behaviours of others around us. There has to be a "me" in the "we" of relationships. When we concentrate on trying to manage the unhealthiness of others at the expense of ourselves then we begin losing the "me" in our emotional worlds and our lives become focused around trying to control others when really these people need to start taking responsibility for their own lives as well as their actions along the way.

Losing Ourselves In Our Self-Image

"I Am Okay If I Look Okay Or The World Reflects Back To Me That I Am Okay."

We live in a social world that validates outside indicators of success. For example, there is a particular prestige that comes with having the ability to wear expensive clothes, drive a nice car, live in a fancy house, and so on. Also there is a prestige in "looking attractive" or dressing up like a professional who appears to have an "important career." In our society, we live in an "impression management world" as we constantly make impressions by how we look, act, and dress.

If we are not careful, we can easily become lost in this impression management world by believing that how others see us in the world is really a measure of our self-worth. In fact, we may believe if others think we look okay then we must be okay. The problem is that these driven needs for validation and outside approval are insatiable. We never quite "look good enough" in comparison to others. There is always somebody with nicer clothes, a bigger car, a more luxurious house and so on.

Also there is an emptiness that comes with not getting enough validation. Some people build themselves up from their accomplishments and feel good so long as they are "achieving." A large part of some people's self-image or how they feel about themselves comes from achieving goals. But what if the goals we set out to achieve cannot be accomplished within our time frame or according to our expectations? What if we do not get that "A" grade in a class at university? What if our boss says "nice job" and not "great job?" What if our business empire we have built has it's lowest quarter in sales ever? As a result we can feel very lost along the way and have an eroded level of confidence as well as self-esteem if the outside world is not "reflecting back to us" that we are amazing or wonderful at any given moment.

In order to gain that outside validation as well as approval, many people will work harder to accomplish their goals or focus on looking even better with plastic surgery. The drive to "be okay" is a consuming one and people can feel very "out of control" inside if they do not feel like the outside world is reflecting back their value and worth. Unfortunately, not everyone will be "wowed" with what we do or how amazing we look. A self-image built within an impression management world is an exhausting way to live as we become "personas" or "walking-taking images" acting like an emotional yo-yo eagerly waiting to see if "everyone is watching us" as they validate how amazing we are. No outside material thing or person can fill up the emptiness we feel within ourselves.

When we live in an impression management world we are grasping at controlling the impressions of others. We position our lives towards gaining status or active approval. In fact, we want people to be "wowed" by our wealth, house, our family, how nice and giving we are, and so forth depending on what area of our lives we are trying to impress others with at the time. We may even believe we "have arrived" in life and work hard to maintain an image that we want others to see in us. In effect we are playing a role in life.

On a metaphorical level, this is much like setting up a projector wheel and a screen while "projecting" an image of how we want others to see us. Meanwhile, we are standing behind the shadows of the screen waiting to see the audience's reaction. If people do not react according to our "wow factor" or praise us with what they see of our image, then we feel out of control as we work harder next time to gain the approval of others. This is a trap whereby we are held hostage and give our power away to the impressions that others have of us. The challenge is to live a life of authenticity whereby we build ourselves from the inside out. We can enjoy successes, but the drive to be okay is within ourselves. Effectively, we are able to unhook from the impressions others have of us and focus on our own lives. We bring God back into the center by exploring His larger design for our worlds and our own callings in life. Therefore, we do not waste precious time riding an emotional rollercoaster of highs and lows worrying what other people think of us. Instead, we step out from the movie screen image of our lives and into the light of who God wants us to be regardless of what people think or say about us. As a result, we are comfortable in our own skin and clear about our direction in life.

The Drive "To Be Okay"

We have reviewed the drive to be okay and how we place our sense of self-worth or self-esteems on externals outside of ourselves. Many of us have a driving belief that "I am okay if others think I am okay" as they become trapped in patterns around people-pleasing. Other people may have a driving belief that "If I can make others okay then I am okay" as they sink into patterns of trying to manage the emotional unhealthiness or acting-out behaviours of individuals in their lives. Finally, some people have a driving belief that "I am okay if I look okay or the world reflects back to me that I am okay" as they become trapped in a desire to have a great self-image within an impression management world.

So where does this drive "to be okay" come from and how does it erode our confidence as well as self-esteems?

The drive to be okay comes from a core emotional experience or series of circumstances earlier in life whereby we felt like we were "not okay inside." We grew up or were shaped by experiences in life whereby we learned that a measure of being okay is for some reason outside of ourselves. For example, we may have had parents or relatives who peppered us with messages that in order to be okay you needed to have a certain income level, acquire a large house, or achieve some type of outside standard. Mark grew up in a family that was middle-class and had a love of money. On family outings his parents always drove through wealthy neighbourhoods admiring the mansions and being "wowed" by the lifestyle of the rich. Mark knew that in order to "be somebody of value", he needed to make lots of money and own one of those mansions because then he had "arrived in life." Essentially, Mark's value came from outside of himself and he was attached to his financial net worth. Therefore, when Mark declared bankruptcy after a business venture failure he had a complete nervous breakdown as he thought that when he lost his finances that he had lost his entire life.

Learning You Are Not Okay Because Of Shame

Many of us grow up in families that use shame as a form of discipline. As young people if we do something displeasing to our parents then we are told that we are "bad" instead of saying we made a "poor choice."

Some examples of shaming comments are:

-"Come on! Think will you! Use that brain in your head!"

-"Is your brain shutting off?"

-"What were you thinking? How could you be so stupid?"

-"I never thought you would do something so stupid ever! You have really disappointed me. I didn't think you were like that!"

With shame we believe that we not only did a "bad thing" but that to some degree we are "bad" as people because of our actions. We live with the formula "I did…therefore I am…" rather than "I did and made a choice that I have learned from and will not repeat again." If we live according to the confines of shame, we are unable to learn from our mistakes and instead we believe we are bad people. The natural process of learning to walk in life involves falling or stumbling along the way. We learn to walk by falling so we are essentially failing our way to success. If we buy into shaming beliefs, then if we fall then we believe we are stupid or incapable of ever learning to properly walk. We feel bad to the core of who we are so we think we are a bad walker in life. It is difficult to step into the confidence of carrying out your higher purpose in life when we become our own worst enemies along the way. Many people have an emotional block around gaining confidence because they have not dealt with the core shaming ideas or messages they have about themselves.

Learning That You Are Not Okay Through Emotional Cut-Off

While growing up we may have been surrounded by people who were extremely moody. In particular a parent may have had an anger management problem so that they were fine and then exploded out of nowhere in anger. Other important role-models may have had issues with mood stability so that they were happy and then suddenly shut down emotionally or crashed into depression. As young people growing up, we may have had to learn quickly how to "navigate around individuals' moods" by adjusting our behaviour to not upset them. We may have learned over time that we could be quite successful in "bringing out the nice side" of this person by shutting ourselves down through "flying low under the emotional radar" of the family by not getting in anyone's way by causing problems. Then once we adjusted our behaviours, this person with the moodiness issue or the instability would start to get better and all would be well for a while until the next incident.

People with mood instabilities participate in "emotional cut-off" (emotional withdrawal) which means that they have a metaphorical "on and off" switch with their emotions. They are either "on" and doing well or they "off" by being angry or depressed. As a result of living in this pattern, we can easily learn that we need to "manage" others or control situations by adjusting ourselves and our behaviours to accommodate their mood instabilities. If we "play nice" or make everything better for the other moody person then all can be well and things can settle down. The problem is that we learn that we can be okay by "making someone else okay first." If that person is moody, upset, and so on then we believe that it is up to us to change our behaviours to make it okay for them. So we may engage in pleasing them or learn to say nothing, deny how we are feeling, and then they will switch back to "being on" or happy again. With such earlier patterns in life, we will become tolerant of other people's emotional unhealthiness. Rather than setting proper limits or boundaries, we will believe that it is our job to make that individual okay first and then we will be okay afterwards. We have a driving need to settle them first in order to enhance our own personal value. If we make them okay then we will be okay.

Another form of emotional cut-off is the pressure "to be good." If we are not a good girl or boy or do not behave like a "good little Christian" should then we may receive emotional withdrawal or distancing from our parents growing up. A standard of proper behaviour is held over our heads and if we "miss the mark" of how we "should" behave, then we receive guilt as well as an expression of major disappointment from our parents. Once we "conform" or do what others expect of us, then we receive validation as well as approval. For example, Nancy wanted to go to a Baptist Bible College upon graduation. Her parents were very disapproving of her choice and wanted her to go to a Lutheran college which they thought had a superior quality of education as well a better reputation. Nancy's parents would not talk to her and she was made to feel like she was a bad person for her post-secondary educational choices. When she struggled for one semester at the Lutheran school then her parents told her that of course she was having problems because she chose the wrong school in the first place!

The result is that we can grow up in life according to a bunch of "should" rules for how we need to think as well as behave. We become very sensitive to the emotional distancing, withdrawal, or disapproval of others and then adjust our behaviour accordingly. Essentially, we need to be okay within other people's standards in order to feel okay inside. In the above example, Nancy would have received her parent's conditional support if she had followed their expectations in the first place.

When The Child Inside Of Us Is Running Our Lives

When we have a drive to be okay that has been interrupted in life with shaming messages or navigating through the moods of others, then this need for self-worth becomes that much more intense. Inside of us becomes a trapped child craving or needing the validation of their emotionally-unavailable parent or responding to whatever other issue was going on at the time in our earlier lives. That emotionally-wounded part of ourselves has a driving emotional need for validation as well as approval and has learned that if he/she can manage a situation, shut down what they think to please others, build an outside successful life, make another individual with emotional issues okay, and so on then inside he/she can be okay.

With some of us, we have an unresolved emotional issue (s) deep within our core that is driving our need to be okay as we attach to external people, material items, status, or image to make us okay feel okay inside. That trapped wounded-child within each of us is running our adult lives and getting in the way of building our core confidence as well as self-esteems. In many ways, we are chronologically moving forward in terms of getting older and moving through emotional milestones like getting married, having a family, building a career, or so forth but we are stuck emotionally and inside of ourselves is a trapped, wounded child needing approval as well as validation.

The Wounded Child In The Driver's Seat Of My Life

Earlier in the introduction I told you about my driving need to build an outside life for myself regardless of what cost it was to my physical or emotional health. I was obsessed with setting goals and accomplishing them to make myself appear successful on the outside while trying to feel okay on the inside.

So why was I prepared to drive myself into the ground at all costs in order to have the career title, the six figure income, the nice house, and the family along with the lifestyle of my dreams?

The wounded child inside of myself wanted the outside world to acknowledge that I was okay inside. I had a shaky inside self-esteem for many of the reasons mentioned above. My father who was an alcoholic had become a sober "dry drunk" with an anger management problem. He had a hair-trigger anger and would explode at any moment. I learned to successfully navigate around "his moods" and the more I would please and try to "bring out the nice side of him", the more he would settle down. I developed a high tolerance for chaos as well as unhealthy behaviours in others and learned somewhere along the way that if I could make others okay, then I would be okay. In fact, as an adult I was attracted to very chaotic people who I could "rescue" as well as fix. If they were "better" as a result of my efforts then I felt like I could "earn" their love and all would be well in my world. I learned quickly that the fruit of saving others with unhealthy behaviours was that I would end up exhausted, depleted financially, and burned-out. There is no reward in serving as a "giver" while surrounding yourself with a bunch of "takers" in this world. People will suck you dry if you let them!

So after giving up "fixing" and "rescuing people" my inner wounded child who wanted so badly for the outside world to say "you are okay" focused on pursuing goals and building a career as well as a family. I worked hard to be successful but the reality was that not many people even cared about "my success." I was a woman in a man's world and people were more interested in how I was raising my children and if I was baking pies properly. I never baked and so I was a failure on two fronts (career and cooking). My frustrated wounded child in the driver's seat of my life then kept focusing on building an even larger outside world. What if I made two hundred thousand a year? That would make me okay inside wouldn't it?

What is your organizing emotional issue that is taking over your life and eroding your self-esteem as well as core confidence in the process? If we do not take a close look at our driving emotional need to be okay and how it is possibly taking over our lives, then we may end up veering off course and losing ourselves along the way. We will attach to outside relationships, the validation of others, and outward success indicators through materialism or status to try and make ourselves okay. Nothing will fill up our emptiness that is of this world. We can try to build ourselves from the outside in and hope that a new relationship, a great job, an unhealthy partner becoming "healthy", or something else can heal up the wounds in our spirits. The reality is that we have to build ourselves from the inside out with God at the center of our lives and then we can step into His higher purpose for our worlds. We are not here in this world to be chasing relationships, managing the unhealthiness of others, or building up a material world to make ourselves feel "okay." The Lord has a higher purpose and it is through adversity, challenges, and suffering which He makes use of which tempers as well as refines us to grow into His design for us. In order to accomplish this we have to look at the foundation of what we build our emotional as well as physical worlds upon.

Chapter 2
The Spiritual Donut

Mathew 7: 24-27

"Therefore everyone who hears these words of mine and puts them into practice is like a wise man who built his house on the rock. The rain came down, the streams rose, and the winds blew and beat against that house; yet it did not fall, because it had its foundation on the rock. But everyone who hears these words of mine and does not put them into practice is like a foolish man who built his house on sand. The rain came down, the streams rose, and the winds blew and beat against that house, and it fell with a great crash."

What foundation are you building your physical, spiritual, as well as emotional world on?

Living In A World Of "Doing"

In this world we have the opportunity to "build" a life for ourselves. This means that we can have identifiable emotional milestones such as going to school, getting a career, getting married, buying a house, having children, saving for retirement and so forth. We have a lot of work to do and if we set our eyes focused on "what needs to get done" then we can be quite successful living in a world of "doing."

While "doing" we have measurable goals and can achieve success as we accomplish these goals. There is a "high" or a tremendous level of pleasure that comes with accomplishing the goals we design for ourselves. Also life becomes more focused because we are determined to complete something with measurable steps involved.

When we are focused on "doing" or "tasking" our way through life, then we become very busy. Time goes by quickly when we are working and we can "get into the zone" which is that flow of contentment that comes from feeling like we are accomplishing tasks.

The trap, however, is that we can lose our core sense of who we are in outside things. Our personal value or "being okay" is outside of us and away from God. We become preoccupied in "building a life" without God at the center of it. If we are not careful, God can become more and more distant from our thinking as we rely on our own self-sufficiency as well as self-will particularly when things are going well in life and we are achieving our goals.

Building Ourselves From The Outside In

We can easily become drawn in to managing situations as we set up variables or look at what we can do to "make things okay." In our quest to "be okay" or "make things okay" we focus on accomplishing our goals. If we have issues in our relationships then our focus may be on "trying to be okay" by "making things okay in our relationships" through pleasing or trying to gain the approval as well as active affection from our spouses. Our attention is focused on action and trying to do something to achieve a result.

On the path of "doing" life, we can fall into the trap of "building ourselves from the outside in." Who we are is defined by outside performance indicators like the success of our job, our house, our family, various material items, status and so forth. We are "filling ourselves up" on measuring sticks around who we are, how we look in the eyes of others, our image and so on. The difficulty is that we are building our worlds on a foundation of sand (Mathew 7:24-27) and when the emotional storms of life come along and "things are not going our way" our foundation is shaken to it's core. We are blown off course, feel out of control, and are vulnerable. In fact, we may not have the emotional fitness or core resiliency to "bounce back" in the face of pain and suffering because the outer worlds we have built up for ourselves may feel threatened. As a result, as a way of coping, we may end up working harder as well as faster as we start "powering our way" through situations while inside feeling like we are "sliding out of control."

Living In A World Of "Being"

The option that we have is to put the foundation of our physical, emotional, and spiritual worlds back on to the rock of God and the Lord's principles for living (Mathew 7:25). We can invite the Lord into the center of our worlds as we bring God back into His rightful place in our lives through a God-led life. Also, we have an emotional core or sense of who we are inside of ourselves. Our emotional core consists of our values, beliefs, personalities, dreams, destiny, legacy, and so forth. This is the "being" part of who we are which is independent of what we do or our actions. We are "who we are" in the full glory of God and we are of His design.

We are "being" in our relationships or in the still moments alone in our thoughts and before God in prayer. When we sit at the edge of a lake reaching out and connecting to the world around us, we are simply "being." Also when we sit and stare into the eyes of a child with all their innocence as well as wonder, we are just hanging out and "being."

When we stop and clear the volume of emotional noise in our worlds, we have the emotional space to "just be" and can then hear the voice of God as we become directed in our lives. Also we are able to transcend out of our "noisy minds" and connect into the full glory of God as He infuses us with strength as well as grace. Essentially, we are filled up from the inside out. The outpouring of blessings in our worlds such as our careers, homes, families, comforts in life, and so forth all come from God as He is at the center of our lives. This way we live in a world where we are built from the inside out and when the "emotional storms of life" or troubles come along we have an inside core from which to draw strength. We are connected to the inner "being" part of who we are as we regroup and regain that core confidence to deal with whatever pain or suffering surfaces in our lives.

The Formation Of The Spiritual Donut

Many of us have the effect of living much like what I describe as a "spiritual donut." We have the outside parts of who we are in terms of the identifiable success markers of the career, house, family, material items and so forth but we are empty in the middle much like a donut. In fact, we may love the Lord with all our hearts but He is not at the center of our lives. If we are to be honest, we have a lot of self-will in our lives as we set our eyes on goals or desired outcomes and "work hard" to make what we desire most happen. God has nothing to do with our thinking and we may do a short, token prayer or "run things" by Him quickly but we are grounded in self-will.

Busyness As The Opiate Of The Masses

In the fallen world, we have a great opiate (drug) or sedative that "numbs us out" or keeps us focused without having to look at the deeper issues of spiritual emptiness in our lives. Our minds are distracted by being busy and "tasking." In particular, in the western world we have an explosion of technology as we can waste away hours functioning on a "mind-numbing level" of blocking out stress and "being busy" through surfing the internet, reading e-mails, staying connected with social networking and so forth. All of these advancements are wonderful and there are several gains we have in terms of building a strong global community through progress in communication as well as connecting all kinds of people towards a common good. I believe that we just need to be careful that we are not living in a "spiritual donut state" and using technology and material items as "stuff" or "empty busyness" which keeps us distracted but does not address the core emptiness that many people feel inside.

In our society, busy people are "important" because they are "on the go" and "have all kinds of things to do." Many individuals are becoming "addicted to busyness" as they overextend themselves and run into such exhaustion that they "do not have time to think." Essentially, busyness has become an opiate of the masses which keeps us focused and as we are bombarded with commercials and messages around how the next new car, perfume, clothes, or electronic "must have" gadget will make us happy. We have the opportunity to keep filling up the emptiness inside of ourselves with stuff or busyness. The spiritual donut is alive and well in our society!

When Addictions And Acting-Out Takes Over

Since many of us have built the foundation of our physical, emotional, and spiritual worlds on a "house of sand", our sense of "being okay" is outside of ourselves and not in our active connection with the Lord. In order to "be okay", we may try to control a situation and make it turn out in our favor to feel that all is well in our worlds. We work harder or faster in order to pursue as well as accomplish the goals we set for ourselves. As a way to feel better, we may focus on the love of our spouse and try to get them to give us attention, provide more affection, or give up their unhealthy behaviours in order to experience the deeper connection as well as validation we need.

When the emotional storms, troubles, pain, crisis, or suffering hits our lives if we "do not feel okay" and without that foundation of the "rock" (God) and an emotional core from which to draw strength as well as confidence from, we feel shaken as well as "out of control." We panic! We freak out! We try and control what we cannot control!

That feeling of "being out of control" or "emotionally-sliding" inside grows in intensity until we feel like we are going to explode. So what do we do with that feeling? We do what we do best which is "block it out" and pretend it isn't there by distracting ourselves.

One way we can distract from the emptiness, percolating emotional currents of unhappiness within ourselves, or the inner feeling of sliding on an emotional level is to get busy! We take on more, do more stuff, run here, run there, and exhaust ourselves to a level of being so bone-tired we don't have time to think! No wonder we are burning out physically as well as emotionally. Many people are "running on emotional fumes" extending themselves everywhere so that they do not have to think all the while letting their own emotional gas tanks run into depletion.

When we do not "feel okay" we also can focus on a "*controlled emotional release.*" The CER (controlled emotional release) is the ultimate "feel good distraction" as we attend to a chemical or an activity that helps us shut our minds down or gives us transcendence out of the stressful state we are experiencing. For a moment we can have a counterfeit experience whereby we convince ourselves that "all is well and perfect" in our worlds.

Below are some examples of common *controlled emotional releases*:

-Sex- using sexual arousal as a type of drug which distracts us from reality. We can get that blast of "feel good" with the adrenaline, dopamine, as well as endorphins and other chemicals in our brains that come with the feeling of being sexually aroused. With lusting, sexualizing others, using pornography, acting-out sexually, and so forth we can "masturbate" or "sexually-release" our problems away for the moment.

-Food- with emotional-eating we can fill ourselves up and enjoy the experience of the food as a way of distracting ourselves from stress. When problems appear overwhelming or we feel like "things are out of control", food is the one thing we can control and immerse ourselves into as a way of mood-altering for a moment until we feel the guilt as well as self-loathing that is common after over-eating.

-Alcohol and chemicals- with alcohol and/or drugs which includes prescription drugs we can "turn down the volume of noise" of overwhelming thoughts in our minds. As a result, we can "take a vacation from our minds", "take the edge off", or "melt away" in a "numbed-out" state.

-Shopping or over-spending of money- we can spend money as a distraction or an escape from our inner unhappiness or emptiness by focusing on the next series of "must have items" as we experience a rush of spending money.

-Gambling- we can focus on the odds of the game and lose ourselves in the outside performance indicators such as the numbers which show us whether we are gaining or not in the quest to "win big" and "master the game."

-On-Line Gaming- we can build ourselves a virtual world and be the star in our own fantasies or games as we avoid daily reality all together. In this world we can be whoever we want as we amass

virtual wealth and power with our video game characters without the natural confines of the real world we live in.

-Compulsive Working- we can lose ourselves in working like a "crazy person" as we immerse ourselves in our goals as well as accomplishments. We are so focused on our goals that we stay on track with these work projects at the expense of our personal relationships. Our "work life" becomes more preferable to "real life" because we have identified tasks, a clear role, and we are able to showcase our successes while following clear measurable goals. Real-life and relationships require emotional demands and do not have clear, identifiable success indicators. Therefore work can become an escape or a "controlled emotional release."

With a focus on a *"controlled emotional release"* to make ourselves feel better momentarily, we are filling up the inner emptiness within with something outside of ourselves. The result is that we get a "short blast" or "rush of feel good" and then we are back into daily life while feeling overwhelmed again. Our brains remember that blast of "feel good" and we want it again because the escape lifts us out of our current lives for a moment, and then after the "high" we feel like we are crashing back to the ground again. We want to be "lifted back up" and out of our problems if even just for a second. This dependency on needing a "lift up" means that we end up constructing an "altered-state" for ourselves over and over again which becomes a type of "escape life." We have a favourite activity or CER (*controlled emotional release*), which we escape to and if we are not careful the CER can start to take over our lives. As a result we begin emotionally-checking out of our relationships because we would rather be with our CER. We avoid dealing with a frustrated spouse who is upset with our lack of attention and instead immerse ourselves into the CER. Why focus on work or our future goals when we can just spend some time doing our CER? Time goes by and hours disappear so we don't have time to do our lists of chores so our responsibilities drop off. The CER becomes more and more important. With addiction and acting-out, we start to organize our days around opportunities for our CRE. Our escape worlds with our CER begins to take over our lives.

We put on "emotional blinders" or live in a type of tunnel vision so that we are focused on our CER and escape worlds without worrying about upsetting others or the negative consequences associated with our acting-out or even possible addictions. As a result, there are red warning flags or signs that we are in trouble. Rather than interpreting these danger signals, we get a rush of excitement because we feel intense. Maybe we will get caught? Perhaps we will spend more money than we have? Will the negative consequences catch up with us? We end up "pushing the envelope" further as we take greater risks and immerse ourselves further into our CER and escape life. Part of the "high" for shoplifters is whether they will be caught or not. Similarly, while balancing on a tight-rope of self-destruction with our CER, we may feel the "rush of teetering on the edge" while completely disregarding the fact that we have put ourselves and our families at risk financially or emotionally because of our obsessions with the escape life or acting-out. This phenomenon occurs when people with sex addictions, chemical addictions, or other problems do a "crash and burn" on the "tarmac of their lives" when the consequences of their acting-out catches up with them.

The Cost Of A "Spiritual Donut" Reality

In a spiritual donut state, we are filling up the "emptiness" or the "void" within by trying to build up our outside worlds with materialism and success indicators, trying to manage situations to make everything on the outside okay so we can be okay inside, or using chemicals as well as habits as part of a CER (controlled emotional release) as a distraction from our sense of overwhelm.

We will be unable to move towards living in the greatest potential of our lives and following our higher purpose according to God's design for us if we are living in a spiritual donut state. Also we will not have the core confidence or emotional fitness to "bounce back" from situations or problems because we are operating within a spiritual donut state. When we get ready to "power up" for obstacles in our lives, we have no foundation to operate from. With the emptiness in the middle, we will either set goals and try to control, "power our way through", or manage situations according to our expectations. We have self-will in the driver's seat of our lives and we will inevitably "drive over emotional cliffs" because we are in fear just trying to deal with whatever is happening according to our own understandings at the time. Our motto in life will be: "When things get crazy just get busy!" We then become the emotional hamster on the treadmill of our lives running faster while burning-out and getting nowhere until we break-down. Another option with managing overwhelm or dealing with problems is to just escape into a CER (controlled emotional release) as our emotional as well as relational lives begin breaking-down because we are in essence starting the process of emotionally checking-out of our lives as the CER gains more ground at the center of our worlds.

The journey towards core confidence is one of "building ourselves from the inside out" so that we invite God back into the center of our lives and build up our core selves as we become equipped for the next chapter in God's design for our lives.

Chapter 3

Emotional Fitness And How To "Power Up" For Anything

When we are faced with pain, challenges, problems, or suffering in life we have to dig deep and find the strength to "power up"! This experience is much like feeling like we are about to be buried by a wave in life. We have to manage the strength to crawl up or at the very least get a leg up or we will collapse under the pressure of the wave and be pounded into the sand! In order to "power up" for challenging situations in life we must "dig deep" into our core being to find that inner strength. People can "say the right things" or make us feel better momentarily, but the reality is that it is up to us to as to whether we will go under with the wave of overwhelm or problems in life. This is a call to the core of our souls and who we are at our deepest levels. As a result, we know "what we are made of" once we have dug deep into who we are and our inner potential for great strength. Emotional fitness is the "bounce back factor" or the ability to "power up" for situations. In essence, we become resilient.

In order to have emotional fitness or the ability to "power up" for situations, my sense of being okay must come from deep within myself at my emotional core.

Shrinking Back Into A Wounded Child

In the last chapter we discussed how a wounded child or part of ourselves that are stuck emotionally can be "calling the shots" or leading the decisions of how we respond to things in life. That wounded child is fearful, wants to control situations, or is driven by a need for love or approval from others that was interrupted earlier in life. As adults, when we are faced with pressure, stress, or even crisis we may feel like we are "shrinking back into a wounded child" state as we lose our sense of personal power or even core confidence. This wounded child part of ourselves may be filled with fear and does not know what to do or is just completely overwhelmed. Now we have the opportunity as adults to love that earlier (or in some cases broken part) of ourselves by telling that wounded child inside it's fine and that the adult inside of us is going to take over. We are going to consciously grow and by digging deep within ourselves we will heal and step into the light within ourselves with God beside us to meet any challenge. God does not give us more than what we can handle.

Finding Me Again

In order to tap into that strong emotional core, we develop the ability to "unhook" from others and their emotional issues. We create a sense of self that is independent of others. In fact, we are not an extension of other people's feelings and emotions. Nor are other individuals an extension of our feelings and emotions. Instead, we all have what is called our *emotional process* which is our feelings, thoughts, and our decisions. Our emotional process and our sense of ourselves is all our own. No one has the right to tell us how to feel or think. We get to be in our own emotional process. Similarly, other people have their emotional processes and they also have the right to feel and think how they want to in life. We cannot control other people's emotional processes and we do not have to be responsible for how they feel. This means that we give ourselves permission to think and feel how we desire and we provide others with a similar freedom by respecting or allowing others to have their own emotional processes.

When I "find me" or my core, I realize in my independence that I have a beginning and end or a sense of self. There is a point where I begin and end and other people begin and end.

This means:

1) I am not an extension of other people's feelings, thoughts, or actions. People do not need to "make me do anything" if I choose not to.
2) I am not responsible for other people's feelings. It is not up to me to make them feel good or bad. If I decide to do something nice then it is my choice and I do not do so out of obligation or guilt.
3) I cannot "make" others feel a certain way. All people "choose" their feelings. I give people permission to have their own feelings. This is one of the greatest gifts God has given us. We get to own our own feelings independently of what other people are doing. We feel because we feel and it is that simple.
4) My feelings come from inside of me. Yes, people influence my moods, but I choose how I react and my feelings follow accordingly.
5) My happiness comes from within me. If I decide to only be happy when "all is perfect in my world" then I may only be happy about three times in my entire life.
6) I am responsible for my happiness. This means that unless I want to be a victim to society, I am in charge of bringing more things or experiences into my life that make me happy while eliminating negativity as well as energy drains from my life "that bring me down."

7) I need to be a "steward over my joy" and by setting appropriate boundaries and limits with others I rigorously protect my inner state of contentment as well as serenity.

Owning Your Feelings

We are covered in pain sensors so that we know instantly when we touch a hot stove that we can burn ourselves. Feelings are our emotional pain sensors. We know that situations with others are good, bad, or even "yucky" because our emotional pain sensors (feelings) react accordingly.

Also when we are in active connection with God we have feelings and the Lord can guide us based on what feels right, peaceful, or good. Essentially, we need our feelings in order to properly navigate through relationships and this world.

We end up having eroded self-esteems as well as confidence issues often because we have fears. Furthermore, people are often all too prepared to tell us that our feelings are wrong or that we shouldn't think or feel a particular way. If we are people-pleasers then we learn how to "shut down" our feelings in order to accommodate others. As people-pleasers we will "talk ourselves out of our feelings" and take on the other individuals' senses of how to think , feel, or be particularly if they are confident. We believe that if others have strong convictions, then they must know what they are talking about so we shut ourselves down accordingly by taking on their views of how things should be.

In order to grow in our emotional core, we must develop a strong sense of self and begin the process of reconnecting back to as well as honoring our feelings independent of what others believe. We have our own emotional process (the stuff that is rattling through our minds and how we feel) and we get to own it! No one should have the power to dismiss our realities, our feelings, and the way we think. This way, we honor our feelings and step into our own personal truth. Our truth does not have to be right, but it is our's to own.

Charter Of Feelings:

1) We get to own our feelings.
2) Our feelings are all our own. They do not have to make sense.
3) There is no truth to our feelings. For example, feelings are not right or wrong. We just get to feel them.
4) Feelings are not good or bad and they are just a state.
5) We need to honor our feelings and they do not have to be explained or justified to others.
6) Feelings are representative of where we are at during that moment in time. With new information or as time passes, we can change our feelings or not.
7) We all have our own personal emotional process that does not have to make sense to anyone else. In fact, we can validate our emotional process and allow people to have their own emotional process.
8) Our feelings do not have to be the same as anyone else's. We do not have to match or synchronize our feelings to others.
9) If others are insulted by our feelings, then this is their choice. We get our feelings and our job is to connect with these emotions for our own healing.
10) When feelings are repressed they become pressurized and leak out in other ways. We need to feel our feelings.

Owning Your Truth

God has provided us with a "gut instinct" or intuition for a reason. Intuition is that guiding voice inside of ourselves or that sense of what we should be doing. With prayer, we can ask God for discernment as well as confirmation around whether a particular path or choice is right. This is the challenge of stepping into God's will for our lives.

If we seek "wise counsel", then the process is around asking people who are solid in their walk with God around what we should do in particular circumstances. The difficulty, however, is that if we "shop for opinions" then everyone will have a different point of view. This is a people-pleaser's greatest nightmare because if they shut themselves down to conform to someone else's truth then what do they do if the next person who comes along has a different perception or truth?

The challenge is to live according to God's will, but also to listen to the intuition He has provided us with in life. We can follow that intuition up with being in active prayer asking for confirmation, reading scripture, seeking wise counsel, listening for God's leadership when He says "No", "Not now", or "Not this way" and so on. We have a "truth" or an intuition for a reason and our sense of how things are and what feels right or not right is up to us to own.

Crazy-Making

The problem that occurs when we are around other individuals with unhealthy behaviours who are acting-out or an in "active addiction" is that they are lying as well as behaving in deceptive ways. Therefore when we "come upon" or discover their lies, they tell us that what we see is not happening or that we are overreacting. If we are people-pleasers, we will second-guess ourselves and conform to their version of reality. Also we may even accept blame for the tension or argument in which we confronted them around their deceptive behaviours. At the end of such disagreements, we may even vow to ourselves to "never bring that up again" as we choose not to confront again in the future. Such patterns are part of a "crazy-making" cycle in which we are told that what we see is not real. Then over time we begin to doubt our version of reality or our truth. The challenge in such circumstances is to re-unite with our intuition, our "gut instinct", and our truth. What we were seeing as well as feeling was real and through another person's deceptions we were in survival mode as well as extreme stress so it was easier to just second-guess ourselves. The truth and gut-instinct we had was always there and we just learned in order to be "emotionally-safe", "keep the peace", and avoid conflict to just bury our truth somewhere along the way.

Your Heart Of Hearts

God has provided us with a "gut instinct" or an inner voice for a reason. This is part of our survival instinct. When "things don' t feel right", we may not know why but we have our intuition or "emotional alarm bells" to let us know that all is not right at that moment. With animals their fur stands up on end when they "sense" that there is danger. Many people also have a similar sensation of the "hair standing up on their necks" or experiencing "butterflies" in their stomachs. This is an indication that something is happening. It is your intuition and it is happening for a reason! God also provides us with mercy and protects us from certain things happening in life by "activating" our intuition or emotional alarm bells.

In order to step into the core confidence of being able to live within our greatest potential or to fulfill our dreams, there will inevitably be people along the way who will not agree with our actions or who will tell us that we are wrong. Many people love to identify limitations for us or "weigh in" on our lives by telling us we cannot do what it is that we want to. The question is whether we are being held back from God's will by other people's negativity or limited thinking? If we are lost in patterns of people-pleasing then we may not have the courage to carry out God's will and His larger design for our lives.

This is where we have an opportunity to live knowing in "our heart of hearts" what is real or true for ourselves. People do not have to agree with us and likely they will not but there is an enormous peace that comes with walking in our own truth and following our "heart of hearts." To thine own self and in God's will be true!

Owning Your Voice

As you become more comfortable with having a sense of self you will realize what is comfortable and real for yourself. As a result, you will be able to not only feel your emotions but express those feelings with phrases like "I feel..." and have a sense of being able to stand on the ground solid in your own two feet. When other people come along and say "No, you don't feel that...you feel this..." or "You shouldn't feel that way...", then as you connect stronger into your core you can "hold steady" in what you think and feel. You now have a voice!

Many people have second-guessed or muffled their own emotional "voices" in life because they were fearful of conflict or they learned early in life to "fly under the emotional radar" and "not cause ripples/waves" of tension in their relationships. In order to step towards our greatest potential in life and into our core confidence, we need to use our voices along the way. Imagine driving a bike down a hill and the brakes do not work. You will need your voice to call out to people to get out of the way for their own safety. If you need to get somewhere in a crowded subway you need your voice to say "Excuse me" as you squish by or you will remain like a packed-in sardine being carried off to another subway station not on your route and you will end up lost as well as off-course. We need our voices in order to navigate through life and in order to get where we are going we need to use our voices along the way.

Using Our Voices In Our Relationships

Relationships are complicated in that there is an agreement or a set of rules of engagement around who has what responsibilities, the division of labor, how much time we spend together, how much emotional space we need, how we can love each other while still having our own goals and so forth. There is much to be negotiated in relationships. If we do not use our voices to share our feelings or declare our needs then we become emotional Siamese twins attached to someone else with no core identity. We just go along wherever that person leads us and we have no voice, identity, or core. In fact, we become a shadow of ourselves.

In relationships the active connection of emotional closeness that we experience is intimacy and this feeling ebbs and flows. Even in the healthiest relationships, we have to work on the connection with each other by actively attending to and spending time together nurturing that feeling. The hope is that the work we do in actively connecting in our relationships is fun as well as rewarding. This way we can stay actively "in love" and not have the foundation of our love eroded through resentments. In order to nourish that connection and to feel fulfilled we need to use our voices to say "What I need is...", "Thanks so much for doing...", "I really appreciate you because...." and so forth. Unfortunately, some people stop "using their voices" along the way because they do not feel heard or validated by their partners and instead they just begin the process of "emotionally shutting-down." Then there are other people who with fear have learned to shut down their voices by pretending that everything is okay when it is not.

Owning Your Value

In life, we will inevitably meet many people who are all too prepared to "toss their emotional junk" over our emotional property lines. This means that in order to get what they need from us they will have no qualms about making us feel guilty if we allow them, taking us for granted, using control as a leverage, attempting to make us feel emotionally unsafe as they activate our fears, and so on. People can be very underhanded and will not respect personal boundaries as they "play dirty" in order to get what they want in this world.

We have the opportunity to sit patiently on the sidelines of life wishing, hoping, and praying that people will be nice to us or do what we want. The reality is that if we allow others to run over us the reward at the end is that we have tire tracks on our backs. Now many people believe that we must "turn the other cheek" (Mathew 5:39). Yes, as Christians we are called to "turn the other cheek" and take the higher ground in our relationships. This does not mean that we are to passively sit and allow ourselves to be treated poorly by rewarding the bad behaviour of others. We are to "rebuke" others particularly when they are sinning (Luke 17:3). Furthermore, Jesus was not passive and instead used his voice as he turned over the tables of the money changers in the temple (Mathew 21:12). We can stand in boldness around what is wrong in life!

We have the option to sit patiently forever as the day is long, or we can start actively changing the nature of our relationships as we "teach people how to treat us." When others are being disrespectful of us, we have the opportunity to "step into our value" and set limits around poor behaviour by drawing "this is not okay lines" in our relationships as we set limits around unhealthiness. With our *feelings* we recognize we are not okay with what other people are saying or doing. As we use our *voices* we communicate the impact of other people's actions on us. In our *value*, we recognize that we will not accept such poor treatment. By standing up for ourselves we change our relationships. The old system of allowing ourselves to receive the "emotional junk" of others is not at play. When we have strong boundaries, people know instinctively what they can and cannot get away with in their interactions with us. We carry with us a core confidence that shines through our being and we communicate the automatic body language that we will not be putting up with other people's "emotional junk." People will throw their emotional litter away and toss their "junk" on to others when they know they will get away with such actions. Much like the bully who "chooses" their victims, people who disrespect others know who they can and cannot mistreat.

In order to step into our core confidence and grow into the greatest potential of our lives we cannot steer that course if we keep tripping over the "emotional junk" people will toss onto our emotional paths along the way. In fact, we may never be able to carry out the Lord's higher purpose for our lives if we continue to allow ourselves to be "buried under other people's emotional junk." We will not see our way out of the emotional garbage that is piling up in our lives.

Healthy Radar

We have a larger responsibility or share for how people treat us. Some of the most powerful people are quiet and have clear limits. As people we all unconsciously know what we can and cannot get away with other individuals. For example, you may instinctively know that this as a person who will not put up with something you do whereas there are others who are more tolerable of poor behaviour. We send a type of "radar" or signals around having clear boundaries as well as limits.

The world reflects back to us how we feel about ourselves. If we feel poorly about ourselves, we will with our "radar" attract people into our lives who are all too willing to treat us badly. With healthy radar, poor treatment feels uncomfortable. We do not send emotional proximity signals (signals of affection or closeness) to individuals who do not treat us well.

People will "meet us in our radar." We are constantly sending signals out in the world around who we are and what we are about. Those signals will be received by others and we will "match" with others in our signals. Poor behaviour from others starts to feel uncomfortable if we raise our radar and only allow people in to be close with us so long as they are respectful and treat us with kindness. This way we are not constantly "tripping over" other people's "emotional junk" in life.

Someone In This World Does Not Like You!

There are very strong chances that you will meet someone or quite a few people in this world who will not like you for whatever reason. Even if you are incredibly nice and try to be overly-accommodating to others, there will be some people who likely think you are "too nice" or even "fake." You can never win and this is why living in your value and according to your truth is such an important part of having core confidence. No matter what we do we cannot make everyone happy. When we give ourselves permission to be who we are and do not live for the approval of others, then we give others permission to be who they are with their emotional processes. We allow people the ability to have their own thoughts and feelings as we acknowledge that we have no control over what people think of us. There is an incredible freedom when we give up trying to control the perceptions of others. When we authentically live according to our values, feelings, and truth then we cannot worry about what other people think. It is nice if other people like us, but we will not die if we do not have the validation of others.

Putting Your Dreams Back On The Board

In the journey of "getting yourself back" you have the chance to settle back into your own independent self. Yes, relational interdependency is a wonderful thing and it is great to give as well as receive love but we are more than just our relationships. We have a self and we are instruments for God's higher purpose in this world. In Romans 11:29 we know that "…for God's gifts and his call are irrevocable." All of us have a larger calling.

The problem is that for many people our larger calling is "interrupted" because of our inner drives to be okay. We have effectively become "emotional yo-yo's" rebounding off of what other people say or do. In our personal relationships we may have even lost our own personal power as we become "captive audience" waiting and watching to see what other individuals will do next. If we are trying to "manage the unhealthiness" of our partners who are "acting-out" or having addictions, then our emotional worlds become smaller as we wait to "catch them in a lie" or spy on them to see what they are going to do as we play out all kinds of potential "what if" scenarios in our minds. Essentially, we are allowing others to serve as emotional vacuum cleaners who have attached their hoses to our happiness, quality of life, and positive energy as we allow them to "suck us dry!" In trying to "manage someone else's unhealthiness", we become unhealthy ourselves.

We can also live a very torturous existence when we feel God's call to do much with our lives and to fulfill His higher purpose which is like a stirring in our souls to the core of our beings but we do nothing because of fear. This is a sensation much like being fuelled with gas or energy and then slamming on the brakes in a stuck position. We feel "the call to drive forward", and yet with fear we are emotionally paralyzed and do not allow ourselves to move forward. Instead, our emotional tires are spinning and the smell of burning rubber is filling the air.

On the journey of "clearing the emotional junk piles" in our lives, we know that our first milestone is to get a sense of self as we learn to own our feelings, truth, voice, and value. This can seem like a daunting task for many people especially if they have been consumed with fear, stress, or have been busy managing the unhealthiness of others. Such individuals may panic when they consider where to even start with this process. In such instances, I recommend creating a dream board.

Exercise:

Get a piece of poster paper and a pile of magazines as a well as scissors and a glue stick. Then begin flipping through the magazines pulling out pictures, phrases, or words that you like or feel like you resonate with along the way. There does not have to be a particular reason why you choose a picture or words. You are assembling a dream board. Start at the center of the board and work your way outwards by gluing down the pictures or words you have chosen. Consider such things as: Who are you at your core? What are your dreams? Make sure you include dreams that do not even appear realistic at this point in time. What makes you happy in life? What fills your soul? What are your priorities? There is no perfect way to do your dream board, but this is an important exercise because what we focus on we create for ourselves in our lives. You are building a positive vision for yourself. By reclaiming back your sense of self and your life, you also clear the path for God to do His work on you and to grow you into His higher purpose for your life. You may feel uncomfortable at times doing this exercise and some people who do this exercise even believe that they are being selfish focusing on themselves. The reality is that unless you get the "me" back in the "we" of your relationships, you will continue to be a shadow of yourself and will not be living according to your greatest potential.

Three Steps Forward and Two Steps Back

So now you have started the process of owning your feelings, truth, voice, and value as you start growing into the potential of your life. As we begin doing this emotional work, we can then start "powering up" for situations as we feel that stronger sense of confidence emerging within. We are in a process of clearing the path of our emotional lives in order to carry out God's higher purpose for ourselves. Along the way, we need to start clearing the emotional path so that we stop "tripping over other people's emotional junk."

You may feel that glimmer of hope inside or that sense that this is possible because things in your life do not always have to be this way, and then suddenly it happens.... out of nowhere you trip and fall! You may feel discouraged like all the hard work you are doing on yourself is for nothing since you are back in the old ways of thinking or mindsets. What you are dealing with is an "emotional trigger" which is an event, situation, or something that happens whereby you react at such an intense level that you feel emotionally lost again. Something has "caught you off guard" and you are reacting big time!

We all have our own "emotional stuff" or areas of our lives that we need to work on. These are all of the unresolved emotional issues or even the parts of ourselves that we need to die unto. Such ways of being are not serving us well and we need to grow on deeper emotional levels in these areas of ourselves. Now we will have partners or other important people in our lives who also have their "emotional stuff" or unresolved issues. In the complication of relationships there will be times when "my stuff" and other "people's stuff" begin to "spark off of each other." There are "emotional triggers" that surface and out of nowhere we may experience overwhelming intensity. These are the times when we can look at our issues and use these situations as opportunities to learn as well as grow on deeper emotional levels as we explore different ways of thinking or reacting on a healthier level. Essentially we are challenged to do things differently or think in alternative ways because whatever we are doing is still bringing up pain for ourselves. In order to shift out of that pain, we are challenged to grow.

Leah's Story:

Leah is married to Mark and he is very moody. There are parts of Mark that need to grow on deeper emotional levels because when he does not hear what he wants to hear or if Leah disagrees with him in any way, then he begins the process of "emotionally shutting-down" or "stone-walling." He will not talk for days and Leah is left guessing what it was that she did that was wrong. As a result, Leah has learned to "walk on emotional eggshells" making sure that she says or does as much as she can to please Mark so that he does not go into "one of his moods."

Leah began to work on her core confidence and felt the courage to stop anticipating whether she was upsetting Mark or not. Her desire in the marriage was to have honest communication which meant that inevitably she would say or do things that were displeasing to Mark. As a result, Mark would begin "emotionally shutting-down" and refusing to talk for days. Then after a while, he would begin talking and this was Leah's cue to forget the issue that had concerned her and then they could pretend nothing happened except that Leah would have to remember not to bring that subject up again.

One day Mark came home from work and before he even said anything, Leah knew he was "in one of his moods." She looked at him and (in her words) "saw the love drain from his face." Leah knew he was in a foul mood, and she panicked. She hid in their room and could feel herself hyperventilating. Mark had never been violent and he was more of a "moody pouter" than anything. As Leah had a panic-attack she felt like she was losing her mind.

What Leah did not realize was that she had experienced an "emotional trigger" from earlier in her life when her mother would do the same thing in terms of "having that look." The difficulty with her mother, however, is that she would explode in violence and then after her outburst pretend there was no problem. Leah was carrying on the same pattern of "walking on emotional egg-shells" and transferring this situation from childhood by re-enacting it on to her husband at an unconscious level. In essence, Leah's earlier wounded emotional child self was in the "driver's seat" of her marriage. Leah was not responding to her husband as the mature marital partner she is today, but instead was shrinking back emotionally within herself into the seven year old girl who was terrified of her mother. Essentially, Leah had experienced "an emotional trigger" (the look on Mark's face) which triggered her unresolved earlier emotional stuff from childhood. Leah was not falling backwards on her journey towards core confidence. Instead, she had experienced an emotional trigger or an indication that there was a part of herself that needed to be brought before God for healing. As Leah grew in her healing journey, more parts of herself that were no longer serving a purpose or helping her as the adult she is today needed to be transformed as well as healed. Leah needed to continue on her journey of growing on deeper emotional as well as spiritual levels as she started healing the wounded parts of herself on the quest towards growing into the greatest potential of her life. Similarly, Mark could not grow into core confidence or his greatest potential until he was prepared to heal the wounded parts of himself that was still behaving like a seven year old child who had an emotional tantrum when people he cared about did not say or do what he expected.

Clearing The Path

We all have a calling (1Corinthians 3:5). In 2Thessalonians 1:11 "With this is in mind, we constantly pray for you, that our God may make you worthy of his calling, and that by his power he may bring to fruition your every desire for goodness and your every deed prompted by faith." In order to complete God's will or higher purpose for our lives, we can be more effective ("worthy of His calling") if we allow God to clear away the "emotional clutter" or "junk" along our paths towards that calling. If we want to grow into our greatest potential for God's higher purposes, we have to be prepared to die unto old parts of ourselves (1Peter 2:24). God refines as well as tempers us like silver (Isaiah 48:10) so that the parts of ourselves that no longer serve a healthy purpose are *burned off* in the process often through affliction.

As we start the journey of owning our *feelings*, *truth*, *voice*, and *value* inevitably "things will come up" and we may experience "emotional triggers." This is a chance where we can use these problems or situations as "teachable experiences" by figuring out what we were doing or saying that is not helpful. Who are we in our greatest potential and who do we want to become? What skills, ways of thinking, or new ways of being can we adopt so that we can manage in a healthier way? As we begin growing, we also see that there is an incredible freedom that comes with handing the old parts of ourselves over to God for healing. The weight of junk along our path in life starts to lighten and we can see the potential of where we are going according to the Lord's larger design for our lives. This is an exciting time because we have an opportunity to walk through life in a different way. We have an emotional core and when we tap into that inner confidence, we not only feel equipped to deal with challenges but we also have a new way of being as we learn not to "go down with the small stuff." In essence, we develop a strong level of emotional fitness. Since we are not constantly tripping we can make large strides forward. We gain effective momentum in our lives and we are unstoppable as we carry out God's will.

Chapter 4
Your Emotional Core

You have learned about getting back a sense of self which means owning your feelings, truth, voice, and value. When you stand strong in that sense of self you can "power up" for any challenge in life. Now the opportunity is to shift from "short blasts" of confidence to having a system or a way of walking through life whereby you can easily tap into that sense of ongoing confidence. This is much like a never-ending well of confidence that comes from the core of who you are and is independent of what is happening in your outside world. Yes, you will still have "bad days" and as people we cannot avoid suffering in life. The difference, however, is that you will learn how to manage once you activate your emotional core and draw strength from inside of yourself. You will have built yourself from the inside out and are not dependent on outside variables with people making you feel better about yourself or needing for things to "go your way." Instead, you can live in freedom knowing that you have the inner emotional fitness and resiliency to manage anything that comes your way.

Also this is an exciting time because as you develop core confidence, you have the added energy to feel like you can manage anything so as a result you are able to see opportunities on the horizon of your life. You no longer live in fear or negativity and with the ability to "power up" you have the added energy to not only meet challenges but see exciting and new creative ways of doing things. In fact, you are effectively able to see the larger design of God's way as He reveals these details as well as opportunities to you. Now you are no longer feeling lost or blinded by fear along the path of life.

So What's The Secret? The answer is core confidence.

Just like how we have a physical core which is the strength inside our bodily frames that carry our body weight, posture, and serves as our strength we also have an emotional core. With emotional fitness, we feel ready to "power up" for whatever situation we are called to attend to in life. The challenge or skill is to "stand in your emotional core" so that you have a solid sense of who you are and you do not attach to other people's comments or criticisms and spiral. Instead, you have an emotional core and stand strong within yourself in your own self-worth.

Your Emotional Fitness Test

There are times in life when we are presented with valleys which are burdens and problems to which there is no instant relief or quick fix. Instead, the challenge is develop the endurance to move through these valleys as we grow on deeper emotional as well as spiritual levels by gaining inner strength and deepening our walk with God. Much like how we have physical fitness levels that consist of flexibility and posture, core muscular strength, as well as cardio endurance we also have emotional and spiritual fitness levels. Are you ready for an emotional fitness test? Ask yourself three questions:

1) **What is your emotional posture towards life?** Do you get overwhelmed easily and struggle to face what appears to be a mountain of issues piling up in your life?
2) **What is your core emotional strength in life like?** Do you have a strong level of core confidence or are you bothered, thrown off, or upset by what other people say

about you? Do you worry about what others are thinking or saying about you?

3) **What is your level of emotional endurance?** Do you get frustrated when things do not settle down and people do not do what you expect them to do?

With emotional fitness we learn the skills to develop inner strength or core confidence so that we gain the endurance to hike through these valleys. As a result we become transformed as well as changed in a positive way through these experiences and we develop a tool box of skills for living along the way. As our emotional fitness levels increase we learn how to "power up" to tackle any issues in life as we develop the core confidence to move through as well as grow on deeper levels through these challenges and closer towards God's overall design of our lives.

Activating Your Core Strength

My sense of who I am has to come from me. I must fill myself up. This is a skill of "standing in my emotional core." I have to have a sense of self or emotional core that is all my own. I am responsible for how I feel. This means I allow myself the freedom to step off of the emotional rollercoaster by returning to "my core." I am responsible for caring for myself, energizing myself, and fuelling or "filling up my core." Furthermore, I operate out of and return back to my emotional core. When I start to spiral or slip, this is an indication that I have to return to my core and start taking care of me. So long as my emotional core is strong, I can live a life with two feet planted solidly on the ground. I become free of other people's expectations and do not worry what other people think. As a result, I have reclaimed myself and my life because I have built myself from the inside out, rather than pinning who I am on the outside and living on this emotional rollercoaster, acting like an "emotional yo-yo" off of what other people say or do.

The Emotional Core

One of the reasons why we are off-center and start to spiral in thoughts of negativity particularly around others is because we have not yet mastered the art of having strong internal emotional boundaries. The skill of feeling balanced, strong, as well as secure regardless of what others say or do is called "standing in your core." Just like there is a "core strength" in physical fitness there is also a core part of ourselves as part of emotional fitness which can be filled with strength as well as resiliency. When we feel challenged to deal with situations we can tap into that inner resiliency or inner core. God strengthens our core and infuses us with strength through His grace.

In order to build our core resiliency and emotional fitness, we must have definite core emotional boundaries. Boundaries are an emotional property line or parameter so that we know how to stand solid in ourselves and not spiral with other people's negativity or issues. We are clear about our individuality and where we begin and end and others begin and end. In fact, we have our emotions and our sense of self and we know with discernment when to not "take on" other people's emotional issues.

Some ways we have weak boundaries around others include:

-We give our power away and second-guess ourselves based on what others say to us about our own potential as well as abilities.

-We please others at the expense of ourselves and struggle with saying "no" or setting limits.

-We allow other people's criticisms get to us.

-We worry about other people's approval of us and how we "look in their eyes."

-We feel guilty or responsible for other people's feelings.

-We allow others to blame us for their problems and we take on their feelings instead of letting them deal with their own issues to some degree.

-We feel like we are a victim to other people's actions. They are "doing things to us" to make us feel bad instead of us taking responsibility for our own feelings/actions.

-We are often upset with others and have problems communicating this frustration with them.

-We are often resentful of others and do not resolve these issues. Instead, we stay mad for long periods of time.

-We have a fear of getting close to others because they may hurt or disappoint us.

-We worry that others close to us are going to reject or abandon us.

-When others are angry, emotionally-withdraw, or shut-down we worry about what we have done and take on their issues trying to make peace because we have fears of conflict.

-We do not get over issues with people or "rebound" back quickly.

Core ResiliencyAnd Emotional Fitness

The ability to rebound back from situations with others, take the learning from that situation, and keep moving forward are the skills involved in core resiliency and emotional fitness. Essentially, this means that we have become "resilient" or that we have the ability to "bounce back" even stronger whenever we have perceived setbacks or challenges along the way. As a result, we can stand strong in our values as well as sense of self. Life does not throw us off-balance regularly. If we have problems, then we work through them. Essentially, we allow ourselves the opportunity to feel various feelings and work through an "emotional process." Each of us have an emotional process which is what we are thinking and how we are making sense of what is happening to us. With core resiliency, we "hold steady" in our emotional process instead of trying to distract or escape from our emotional issues.

With resiliency and emotional fitness, we can "hold strong" in being open to what people have to say and what they think, but we do not lose ourselves in negative thought spirals over what they say or do. For example, everyone has an opinion and their version of truth. When we are resilient, we "hold steady" in what we believe by being open to new learning, however, we are clear with ourselves around what we truly believe. Therefore we can "allow" people to have their opinions, and can be respectful of differences but we do not begin shutting ourselves down to conform to other people's versions of reality.

Furthermore, by becoming resilient we end the cycle of serving as "emotional yo-yos" with continuous highs and lows, rebounding off of what other people say or do. We are not so quick to "give our power away" and allow others to destabilize us. Also, with emotional resiliency we are able to manage any sense of overwhelm in life. We know that we can break down tasks, develop clarity, and are able to distinguish between our own issues and other people's issues. This means that we all have "emotional backpacks of stuff" that we are carrying. In these emotional backpacks are unresolved issues or emotional issues we are struggling with along the way. With resiliency and emotional fitness, we are clear about what is our own "emotional backpacks" to carry and we feel equipped to deal with "our stuff." Also we are clear that we do not have to start carrying around other people's "emotional backpacks" as well as our own. Instead, we allow others to have the "gift of owning" their emotional back-packs as they work through their own emotional processes to grow on deeper physical, emotional, as well as spiritual levels. We "own" our parts in situations and manage what we can do on "our side of the street" while giving-up or letting go of trying to control what others do.

What does an emotional core consist of?

LIFES

In order to "activate" your emotional core or inner strength, there are five dimensions of your emotional core. Our emotional cores are much like "an emotional as well as spiritual energy battery" or a "well of confidence" deep within us which we can activate as well as "operate out of" in order to "power up" for situations in our lives. The five dimensions can be broken down into the acronym "LIFES."

L:Core lovability

My ability to love myself and feel God's love for me which is independent of what is happening in the world or how I am viewed "in the eyes of others."

I: Identifying myself through the seasons

My story of who I am in this world and who I have been all along as I continue to evolve.

F: Filling myself up

My understanding of what energizes me and brings me joy as I focus on my dreams, goals, and passions in life.

E: Expression of self

How I am able to express myself and create my mark on my surroundings or environment.

S: Spiritual connection

How God utilizes me and my gifts as I have a sense of giving back.

When I have activated my core and opened up the abundant well of confidence deep within myself, I am truly able to "like myself". As a result, I step into my value and allow others to love me in a healthy way. Poor treatment from others feels uncomfortable. I know that I am okay no matter what. In fact, I step into this ability to give myself permission to be who I am. When I give myself this permission, I then give others permission to be themselves. I have core confidence to deal with situations in life as they arise and I do not have to try to manage outcomes of circumstances or furiously control what is going on around me. Instead, I become clear around what I can influence and what I cannot ultimately control. As a result, I engage in a process of surrendering control as I walk alongside God with the Lord at the center fully equipped to carry out His larger design or higher purpose for my life.

Dimension One: Core Lovability

My ability to love myself and feel God's love for me which is independent of what is happening in the world or how I am viewed "in the eyes of others."

One of the major reasons why we do not rebound back quickly from problems or we "lose ourselves" along the path of life is because we have a misplaced "drive to be okay." Our sense of being loved or validated comes from outside of ourselves in that we need to be actively affirmed "in the eyes of others." The problem is that people will inevitably disappoint us because human beings are by their very natures fallible or have faults. When we get into emotional tangles or have challenges with others, then many of us are all too prepared to "give our power away" by hoping that these people we care about will see the error of their ways and return back to a baseline of actively affirming us by apologizing as well as ensuring they do not make mistakes again. Such expectations are unrealistic because of course pride gets in the way even if people are wrong. If we wait for others around us to naturally see the "error of their ways" we will be sadly disappointed. More often, people do not accept blame and may even decide to point fingers at us by mentioning all the mistakes we have done in life as well.

As a result, if we do not have a strong sense of self that is independent of what other people think, say, or do then we will become "co-pilots" on other people's "emotional rollercoasters" which means that we will feel highs (when we are getting active affirmation) and lows (when there are problems). If we need others for validation, then we will have constant highs as well as lows as we rebound off of whatever is happening in our environments at the time. The challenge is to have an internal state of "holding steady" or "being okay" no matter what.

One way to reach that sense of inner serenity is to feel a sense of "core lovability" which means knowing that to the very core of who you are that you are lovable. Even if people in your life are mad at you right now, this does not negate your lovability as a person. You are lovable and are worthy of love. When we have "core lovability" we are not so prone to "tripping" on the path of life. People cannot destabilize us because we are not running circles around them trying to get their attention, validation, or affirmation. Furthermore, individuals cannot "hold power" over us by withdrawing this love either until we do whatever it is that they want at the time. With core lovability we do not "get hooked" into other people's issues and do not have an overwhelming desire for approval. It is nice that other individuals love us and are actively providing love as well as attention, but we do not "lose ourselves" in the "care" we are receiving. Instead, we *want* to be with people in our relationships as that is the "icing on the cake" of life and our lives are enhanced tremendously with their company, but we do not *need* to be with them. We will not die if people do not give us active attention as well as affirmation every moment of the day.

Rather, we know deep down into our souls that we are lovable regardless of what people say or do at any given moment.

If we are in an argument, even if we are unhappy at that moment we still know we are lovable. Also if someone we care about has unhealthy behaviours such as "acting-out" or addiction, we know that we are still lovable and we allow those individuals to "own" their issues. Other people struggling with addictions do not have these problems because of us. We know we are lovable independent of their problems.

Our ability to feel lovable starts at the core of who we are and is within an active relationship with God. We are not alone in this life. Instead, the Lord has "chosen" us for His higher purposes and He breathes life into us as well as moves through our lives on multiple levels. He is in everything and with His love we can do anything (Psalm 18:29). This is a journey of faith that reaches into the souls of who we are as people.

Why are we lovable in God's eyes? There are at least seven reasons.

Reason #1: God chose us personally and He designed a life for us.

God sent his only begotten son to us to lead the way to salvation.

John 3:14-17

"Just as Moses lifted up the snake in the wilderness, so the Son of Man must be lifted up, that everyone who believes may have eternal life in him. For God so loved the world that he gave his one and only Son, that whoever believes in him shall not perish but have eternal life. For God did not send his Son into the world to condemn the world, but to save the world through him."

Hebrews 7:27

"Unlike the other high priests, he does not need to offer sacrifices day after day, first for his own sins, and then for the sins of the people. He sacrificed for their sins once for all when he offered himself."

Reason #2: God predestined us for his adoption.

Ephesians 1:4-5

"In love he predestined us for adoption to sonship through Jesus Christ, in accordance with his pleasure and will-"

Ephesians 1:11

"In him we were also chosen, having been predestined according to the plan of him who works out everything in conformity with the purpose of his will,"

Reason #3: God so loved us that he "called us out of darkness."

1Peter 2:9

"But you are chosen people, a royal priesthood, a holy nation, God's special possession, that you may declare the praises of him who called you out of darkness into his wonderful light."

Reason #4: The Lord rejoices over us out of His love.

Isaiah 49:13

"Shout for joy, you heavens; rejoice, you earth; burst into song, you mountains! For the Lord comforts his people and will have compassion on his afflicted ones."

Isaiah 62:5

"As a young man marries a young woman, so will your Builder marry you; as a bridegroom rejoices over his bride, so will your God rejoice over you."

Isaiah 64:8

"Yet you, Lord, are our Father. We are the clay, you are the potter; we are all the work of your hand."

Reason #5: God wants an interactional relationship with you.

Zephaniah 3:17

"The Lord your God is with you, the Mighty Warrior who saves. He will take great delight in you; in his love he will no longer rebuke you, but will rejoice over you with singing."

Reason #6: God provides us with strength and sustenance.

2Samuel 22:29

"You, Lord, are my lamp; the Lord turns my darkness into light."

Reason #7: We are not alone. The Lord walks with us through the world. He is in everything.

Psalm 23

"The Lord is my shepherd, I lack nothing. He makes me lie down in green pastures, he leads me beside quiet waters, he refreshes my soul. He guides me along the right paths for his name's sake. Even though I walk through the darkest valley, I will fear no evil, for you are with me; your rod and your staff, they comfort me. You prepare a table before me in the presence of my enemies. You anoint my head with oil; my cup overflows. Surely your goodness and love will follow me all the days of my life, and I will dwell in the house of the Lord forever."

Walking Through Life With God's Love

We can take the infusion of God's love and bring it into the core of our being. We are worth something, we have a purpose, and we are not alone. So what does that mean to transfer that sense of love we have from God into our core?

This means:

1) Do not lean on your own understanding (Proverbs 3:5). God has your back. Step into faith and draw close to Him regardless of your circumstances. The Lord has a larger reason or story for why things are happening the way they are right now. It will all make sense later. Draw closer to God for strength in spite of your own thinking or understanding right now.

2) We have to truly love ourselves in order to love others. When we stand in God's love and "own" our core lovability then we enter into a process of being able to give as well as receive love with an open hand. We no longer live in fear and our relationships become more healthy. In fact, we know we are worthy of love and poor treatment from others feels uncomfortable. As a result, our relationships change for the better because when we stand in our own sense of love for God and respect for ourselves at our core, we have a sense of value. Now we can "invite" people to "meet us in our value" by having proper boundaries so that we ensure we are treated kindly and with respect at all times.

3) If God has a purpose for us and loves us and has made the ultimate sacrifice then we have the ability to esteem ourselves. We are here to glorify God and not to run circles around others trying to get their validation as well as approval. We have the opportunity to "step into the worthiness" of the "calling" God has for us (2Thessalonians 1:11).

4) We do not give others the power to leverage withdrawal of affection and love over us. In fact, when we feel our "core lovability" we begin to "raise our value" so that we have limits and teach people how to treat us. We do not put up with poor behaviour.

5) No matter what is happening around us, we know that we are loved and are lovable.

The Walk Of Self-Respect With God At The Center

We have an opportunity to actively draw down an infusion of God's love into who we are by accepting as well as embracing the Lord's grace into our core. We are then able to *step into the light* of the Lord (1Peter 2:9). Once we are infused with that sense of God's love we can build a foundation of personal respect for ourselves. If God "chose us" and this was predestined, then he also planned every part of us for a reason. When we stand in personal respect for ourselves with God at the center of our lives, then we are prepared to "take what we have" and make it work for ourselves. There are beautiful parts of ourselves and there are some "not so beautiful parts" or areas for improvement according to different standards. Regardless of the imperfect parts of ourselves, with core lovability we have self-respect and we make these parts "work for us." You are the way you are with the circumstances you have and it is not by accident. God is interacting and weaving a tapestry through your life.

If you were to take off all of your clothes and stand before a full length mirror what would you see? Would you start instantly "tearing yourself apart" on an emotional level by having your eyes gaze at all the imperfect as well as flawed parts of yourself? Does Summer and "swimsuit season" terrify you to your deepest levels? When we have self-loathing or parts of ourselves we feel we need to hide, then we are giving up our personal power to others and their standards of approval or disapproval. Our imperfections are there for a reason and are part of God's larger design as well as function and purpose. Even so called "ugly fat, sausage toes" give you balance to walk properly. You can cover long distances with "seriously ugly" feet and they serve a purpose. With self-respect, we are grateful for that purpose and give glory to God that we have feet to criticize in the first place.

Shining In The Light

Our personal beauty is much like a light that comes through us from within our core. The cultural standards of beauty have much to do with symmetry and balance in terms of the spacing of people's eyes, noses, mouths, or overall proportions as well as cheekbone structure and skin complexion. Our western culture values small waists, long legs, large breasts, and so on. Beauty really is, however, the "ability to come alive." Have you ever seen people who were "full of life" in that they had a laugh that was adorable or that they carried with them "an energy" that filled the room in a positive way? Such individuals are vibrant and their "positive energy" is contagious.

All of us "shine in the light" when we are happy and feel inspired by our passions, dreams, as well as goals. With energy as well as excitement, we become captivating. I have an amazing group of girlfriends and when we get together my face literally hurts for hours afterwards and my stomach is strained from so much laughter. We are a "bunch of goofballs" who "spark off" of each other in silliness as well as fun. This group of ladies love to laugh and have a good time. When each of them talks or makes a joke, their eyes light up and they are beautiful. I will look at them "in their light" and notice details like how shiny their hair is, how their eyes sparkle, or their smiles as they say something so hysterically funny that I am about to fall out of my chair with laughter. These women are beautiful to their very core and they are wonderful mothers to their children as well. While joking around, I love to "jump in" and "stir things up" as I feel very alive as well as vibrant around them. My core lovability comes out in this crowd of gals and we have a nice chemistry together as friends.

So what is beauty and why do we tear ourselves down because we do not meet "supposed" cultural standards?

Okay, so let's do an experiment. I'll pretend I am standing beside a "hot", young 19 year old yoga instructor. She meets the cultural standards of beauty in that she has that small waist, long blonde hair, large blue eyes, breast implants, long legs that she can extend over her head, and a very soft, high pitch voice if only a Barbie-doll could speak. Then there is me. At the time of writing this book, I am 42 years old, I have given birth to three children, my metabolism is slowing down and if I am going to eat that plate of pasta then I better get up out of my chair and walk around my block at least three times before I even think of eating it. I have arthritis and my neck is completely fused. It doesn't move. So I won't be extending my legs over my head any time in the near future. I also have the joy of gray hairs coming in and there are those thick razor-like black hairs that after a certain age start to grow out of your chin or the side of your face for extra fun. In fact, I keep noticing those hairs every once and a while usually after being out in public all day so if people looked close they could have seen those beauties hiding somewhere in my complexion.

So who has more value me or the 19 year old yoga instructor? We all have value. The yoga instructor "wins" according to sexual desirability and the western cultural standard of beauty. When I stand in my core lovability, however, I know I am living in dimension. My beauty shines from within me. I may have lines forming on my face, but I have lived. I know what it is to love and to have lost. I am there to hold my daughter while she cries inconsolably because her friend has "broken up with her." My heart aches, but I am alive. I am my husband's best friend and his emotional equal. We have travelled the world together and laid on the bottom of the ocean while scuba diving in the Great Barrier Reef of Australia (in Cod Hole) rolling around with 500 pound grouper fish called Potato Cod who like to snuggle and have their chins rubbed. We have dived with sharks who were fed tuna heads on a chain. When my husband shares with me something that happened in the "80's", I get it. I was there and I understand him. My husband has a partner in which to stand beside in life and not to stand on. I will never be "arm candy" or a "trophy." I am inexplicably me and I am "weird." My husband actually "digs" my "weirdness" and meets me at that level and we love to laugh!

Take What You Have And Make It Work For You

Earlier I mentioned ugly feet. Well I have a confession, my toes are ugly. Not just a little ugly, but really ugly according to western cultural standards. At the age of 25, my arthritis had already started in my body. Also at that time my "maternal clock" started sounding. Not just a little sound, but a roaring blare that almost consumed my life. I wanted a baby! My husband and I were not together yet and so I resolved myself to the fact that I would wait until my thirties or whenever but that I would buy a "furry baby" in the meantime…a large breed Doberman pincher who was all too prepared to serve as my surrogate baby. She was beautiful and her name was Chelsey, all 119 pounds of her. The problem was that Chelsey loved to hurl her body on to the couch when the mailman knocked at the door to deliver mail as she would try to look out the window barking loudly and she also had a passion for jumping on people's toes in excitement. This was very unhelpful for someone like me with arthritis because as Chelsey jumped on my toes, my bones in my toes were fragile. Essentially, Chelsey munched my toes and permanently dinted them. So every time I take my shoes off, I look at my feet and think "wow, toes you really are ugly!"

Now if I stand in self-respect and connect with my core lovability with God at the center of my life then I need to be okay with my ugly toes and maybe even provide glory to the Lord for having these indented stubby features at the ends of my feet. So what do I do when my automatic reaction is to "tear myself apart" with criticism? Well, I make my toes work for me. I embrace them and all of their ugliness. When I see the indents, I giggle and think of Chelsey. I also thank God for unanswered prayers in that I did not marry my boyfriend at the time I had Chelsey and so badly wanted a baby. Instead the Lord cleared my life by growing me into who I am so that I was "ready" for my husband to come along after that previous relationship ended. Also, I am very grateful because with my toes I can balance and when I get excited talking I lift up on my toes and start to do a funky little dance/wiggle which makes my husband laugh. I am sure I look very "dorky", but it is fun.

So how can you "re-story" parts of yourself and take what you have to make it work for you?

In your core lovability, you give yourself complete permission to be who you are in all of your completeness. You are not an accident and everything serves a purpose in God's overall design. By having self-respect you treat yourself with kindness and do not "beat yourself up" or tear apart your self-esteem. You do not have to serve as your own worst enemy. Instead, you can step into the completeness of who you are with your core lovability.

Your Purpose Is In Being An Instrument Of God

As you settle into your core lovability, you will realize that it is important to get out of God's way so that He can do His work through you. In fact, you are adopted by him for His higher purpose so the words you say, the ways you treat others, your ability to help, and so forth can all be used for God's greater purposes. Essentially, we are instruments of God and are not here on this Earth to try to conform to having certain sized waists or particular bra sizes. Likely, God is more concerned with the words we use and the hands we have to help others. Jesus talked about the second commandment of loving your neighbor as yourself (Mathew 22:39) so through our interactions with others when we are kind, we are ultimately serving God.

You are a channel for God's light. So long as you have a body, it is beautiful. When we take the "flawed" parts of ourselves and use them to glorify God then we are able to "unhook" from the snare of self-loathing and get off the road of vain self-glory. We have the opportunity to "settle into ourselves" and have God move through our lives by using us as an instrument of the light for His purposes. There is no greater honor.

Now some people are resistant to wanting to give glory to God because out of their flaws or circumstances they have experienced great suffering. There was a time when I was so crippled by my arthritis that people on ferries would stare at me perplexed at why someone who was so young was walking in such a compromised fashion. They would look at me to see if I had any indications of having cerebral palsy. Strangers would ask me, why was I walking like that wondering if I had just been in a bad car accident? I felt humiliation as well as shame. In the ability to tap into my core lovability, I had a chance to take these circumstances and make them work for me. How do you make lemonade out of lemons? It is through those experiences that I really learned to let go of my self-image and the need for validation of physical beauty. I felt unfeminine and I leaned on God for strength. The Lord filled my soul with grace and I developed an incredible level of perseverance independent of what people think of me. I learned during those days to not care what people think because if I could get out of bed relatively pain-free, it was a good day. Now with knee replacement surgery, with so many steps and regained mobility I praise God each and every day. The deeper character trait of not caring what people think of my physical beauty still remains which is a great quality of confidence to have in life.

When we experience suffering or pain, we have the option of becoming gardeners in that we can turn the "crap" in our lives into fertilizer to grow towards God's higher purposes and His will for us. My voice, words, and deeds are more important for carrying out God's purpose than how I look or how people respond to me. In fact, with core lovability, my value is not in my body. Instead, my body is there to carry out deeds of action for God's purposes. When I surrender my ego, I experience tremendous freedom. People no longer have the ability to "hook" me into their approval or disapproval. I am able to live for my own truth independent of what people think of me.

Don't Lose Your Lovability In Other People's Unhealthiness

Let's get something straight which is a misconception for many people. As individuals, we cannot "make people feel" or "cause people to do things." With our free-will as autonomous human beings with brains we all have the ability to choose our feelings and our actions. We are not powerless over how we feel and if we adjust our thinking about issues we can actively change our feelings. All of our emotions flow out of the thoughts we have in our minds. Change your thoughts, then you change your feelings as well as your reality!

Now when we are in relationships with people who are struggling with their own issues with "acting-out" (being self-destructive or dishonest) or who have addictions, then these individuals are all too willing to hand the responsibility of their lives over to others. For example the alcoholic will say: "Well of course I had to drink because you made me mad." Then the partner of the alcoholic learns to not say or do the wrong thing to make him mad out of fear that he will drink. The alcoholic drinks anyways and now has the ability to do so because the partner has agreed to give him the necessary emotional space as well as distance so that he can drink freely by himself without question.

So when a spouse "acts-out" with pornography or any other issues, a typical response for many partners is to blame themselves as if something they did "caused" those people to have problems. Unfortunately, we are not that powerful. We cannot "make" anyone do anything. All people choose their feelings as well as responses. As adults, particularly in a court of law, we have to take responsibility for our decisions along the way especially if we break rules or even laws.

Some spouses will have affairs and partners often feel that it is because of their "unlovability" that they were never good enough so that is why these spouses "went outside of the marriage." Similarly, partners of people with porn issues often feel that it is because of their body flaws or lack of sexual appetite, that their partners went outside of the marriage to meet their sexual needs. The reality is that people arrive in their marriages with unresolved emotional issues. A spouse having an affair does not mean that their partner is unworthy of love. No one can "push" someone to act-out with an affair. This is a choice for spouses who are unfaithful.

Sometimes people are incapable of appreciating our lovability because their own unresolved emotional issues are in the way. Such individuals cannot "see" our value even if they are married to us. It is not our lovability that is at question. Instead, these people are lost in their own emotional issues and our "goodness" cannot "heal the brokenness" in others. This idea that we can make bad people good or that we can bring out the nice sides of them to grow them into their potential because of our great qualities is the formula script material that romantic Hollywood movies are made of in this world. The "Beauty" cannot make the "Beast" want to be a better person and see his inner glow. We are not in a Disney movie like "Beauty and the Beast" and are instead in real life. At the end of the day, everyone gets to take responsibility for their own actions and will have to hold an account before God (Hebrews 4:13).

With core lovability, we know we are lovable and we allow others to "own" their own issues as they work their process of recovery or healing. We are clear about our issues and deepen our walk with God so that we give up the parts of ourselves that do not serve a purpose and that we must die unto (1Peter 2:24).

If people cannot "see" our value or our core lovability, it does not mean that it is not there. Often people who are struggling with unhealthiness in their lives will marry partners who are very healthy as well as high-functioning. Such unhealthy individuals hope that through osmosis that married life will make them normal or heal their deeper unresolved emotional issues. These people come to their marriages "broken" and have not healed the earlier "wounded" parts of themselves. Unfortunately the "acting-out" or "addicted" behaviour escalates in marriage as partners become preoccupied with the needs of the children and responsibilities are more emergent in these overall relationships. There is nowhere to hide and the unresolved emotional issues long buried within people percolate to the surface of marriages. As a result, healthy partners often feel like they have "caused" this unhealthiness especially since issues that may have not been obvious before are glaringly apparent in married life. We all have our own emotional issues likely around people-pleasing, not having clear boundaries and so forth but we are not "causing" our partners to have emotional affairs, engage in pornography, act-out sexually, compulsively spend money, and so forth. With a sense of core lovability, we give ourselves "permission" to let others "own" their issues and we become clear around the emotional housecleaning needed in our own lives.

When People Can't "See You"

In my twenties, I had a brief relationship with a man and then he dumped me. My ego was crushed. He was thirteen years older than myself and he was the only "older man" I had ever dated. In the midst of the "dumping", he told me that I was boring and that I depended on him for excitement. In his opinion, I did not have a life outside of him and he could not handle the pressure of this responsibility especially since we had been dating for eight weeks. I reeled in shock when he said this to me because I had enrolled in a Masters Degree program in Counselling Psychology to train to become a registered clinical counsellor and I was leaving in six days for a two month trip travelling through South East Asia by myself. I didn't think that was boring. This man had the inability "to see" my value or me. He didn't know me to the core of who I was nor could he ever appreciate me in my full dimension. While travelling in South East Asia, I had a dream about him and there was a curtain separating me and him. From the hem of the curtain an abundance of pearls kept dropping on to the floor before me. I saw the pearls in my dream and was excited as I began scooping them up in my hands. Afterwards, I awoke and thought about the dream as I realized I was reclaiming my "pearls" or my value from him. At that point in time, I vowed to myself that I would never cast pearls before swine who could not appreciate them. Now I am not calling him a pig, but I am using the example of pearls of value and how a swine could not appreciate them. He could just as easily be a beautiful dog, a horse, and so forth who still could not see the value of my pearls. In Mathew 7:6 Jesus reminds us "Do not give dogs what is sacred; do not throw your pearls to pigs. If you do, they may trample them under their feet, and then turn and tear you to pieces." Therefore if people do not *see your value* or *see you in your full dimension* or core lovability, do not cast your pearls before them. Instead, *stand in your value* as well as self-respect as you cast your pearls before others who recognize you and will *meet you in your value* by treating you with kindness.

Be a steward over your lovability and preserve it. Do not let other people mistreat you and do not give your power away! With core lovability, you secure your love from God and with the infusion of His grace you feel secure. Your love from God and the infusion into your spirit of that love is one of your greatest resources. It is the casing of your energy battery or the walls of your well of confidence. Don't give or sell it away to anyone! Don't beat yourself up! Stop being your own worst enemy.

Don't engage in internal warfare and tear yourself down. With core lovability, we "unhook" from people's unhealthy issues and we step into the light into God's larger design for ourselves. We give ourselves permission to just show up for life in whatever state as we are ready to be instruments for God and His higher purpose. Furthermore, we know we are loved and are not alone.

When you give people the power to determine your lovability and value, you will do an emotional tail-spin or downward spiral. Instead, with a sense of core lovability you can be prepared to not "wear" other people's issues and let them "own" the responsibility of their decisions. There is the option of not allowing other people's emotional issues to erode your own self-esteem. In essence, I let people love me but I do not give my power over to them. I reclaim my lovability and keep in mind what is lovable about me. This way I can step off the emotional rollercoaster once and for all as I walk a straight path in God's light and love.

The ingredients for self-respect are:

RESPECT

R-Raise your value
E-Esteem yourself
S-Stand in your emotional core
P-Point out the "this is not okay line" or limit
E-Expect healthy treatment from others
C-Control your reactions and work towards being calm
T-Turn towards your truth and honor your emotional process

Dimension Two: Identifying Yourself Through The Seasons

My story of who I am in this world and who I have been all along as I continue to evolve.

One of the reasons why we lose our confidence is that we allow other people to "weigh in" to our lives or introject their truth of who we are on to us. Individuals who do not have very good boundaries may even say things like: "I know you better than you know yourself." If we are people-pleasers then we are in trouble because we are likely to start second-guessing ourselves when we encounter others who are confident about "who we really are."

Everyone has a story or version of truth as well as opinions. Some people stand confidently in their opinions and they are very adept at trying to get the rest of the world to see things like they do on many levels. The problem is that if we destabilize or start second-guessing ourselves when confronted with the confidence of others, then we are going to get distracted from rising to our greatest potential and developing core confidence. We will doubt ourselves and try to conform to whatever other people want us to be or we will adopt their way of thinking in order to gain their approval.

An important part of developing core confidence is to "hold steady" in our own truth of who we are as people. Nobody knows you better than you know yourself. You are only as predictable as you decide to be at that moment. People will be full of all kinds of opinions and they will evaluate us as well as determine our value in their eyes. We live in a world filled with judgments. Some people even feel better by living in a "crabs in the bucket phenomenon" whereby if they see someone getting ahead (much like a crab trying to crawl out of a bucket), they try to "pull them down" (just like crabs who pull the other crawling crab down.)

Introjection is the process of people inserting their ideas of who we are on to us through the leading questions they ask in an attempt to get us to conform to their reality.

For example:

Jessie and her husband lead the youth team. Jessie's husband is the Youth Pastor. Unfortunately Jessie's husband has been struggling with depression and has stepped down from his position to take a leave for a while. People in the congregation want to know what happened to Jessie's husband but they are too afraid to ask, yet they have their "suspicions." Linda (the wife of an elder in the church) is a little braver than most individuals and the "talk" around the church is that Jessie is an unruly wife who is not supportive of her husband. People believe she is not "strong in her faith" and is jealous from all the time her husband has been devoting to the youth ministry.

Linda asks: "So Jessie how are you? How are you r.....e....a... ..l....l...y?"

Jessie says: "Okay and you?"

Linda: "Well actually I am not doing well as I am really concerned. Is everything okay with you and your husband?"

Jessie: "Yes, he is just going through some stuff right now. He'll be fine."

Linda: "Yes, stuff I have heard. How are you managing? My understanding is that you have stuff going on as well."

Jessie: "Stuff, what do you mean?"

Linda: "Well it is often very difficult for wives of ministry leaders to support them wholeheartedly you know...."

Jessie: "I support my husband, what do you mean?"

Linda: "Well, we often say we support in words, but are we really supportive in our actions?"

Linda keeps leading Jessie into an emotional corral to try and get her to conform to her version of reality. With leading questions, Linda is trying to get Jessie to admit she is controlling and has issues with her husband's leadership in the ministry. The truth is that Jessie's husband is battling depression and has lost his drive to work with youth. He is stressed out and is considering leaving the ministry all together. Jessie has been the one trying to convince her husband to go back to what she believes is his calling in working with youth. Overall, Jessie knows "the truth" of their circumstances but has found herself in a situation whereby she is having to explain her reality to someone else who is convinced otherwise.

In the second dimension of our emotional core, we are able to identify ourselves through the seasons by sorting out our truth around who we are and what we are about in life. We all have an underlying narrative or story around our own capabilities, who we are, how the world operates, and how we fit into the world. It is important that we stand strong in our sense of self and the positive story we have about ourselves. There will inevitably be people like Linda in the example above who with great confidence will try to introject their version of reality on to us. Such people will come along and try to "place us in an emotional box of their understanding." These individuals "do not see us" in our full dimension and if we do not have a solid personal story of who we are in life through the different seasons, then we can easily begin second-guessing ourselves or even destabilizing (going off our emotional centers) because of their negative influences and desires to "weigh in" on our lives.

Furthermore, we can easily feel like we are "held hostage" as a captive audience sitting there listening to someone introject their truth of who we are on to us. If we are a people-pleaser, then we will feel trapped as if our only choice is to "just take it" as we nod in agreement while screaming inside of ourselves. Then we may even walk away wrestling with this person's version of reality as we begin second-guessing ourselves. In the above example Jessie may walk away from her conversation with Linda knowing she is not trying to control her husband or being an "unruly wife", however with Linda's sense of confidence as well as truth Jessie may begin second-guessing her motives in her own marriage as she starts conforming to Linda's version of reality. Instead, Jessie can "know herself through the seasons" and have a strong sense of who she is in life so that her story of herself (she knows herself better than anyone) is independent of what Linda ever thinks about her. Also, Jessie is not a captive hostage to Linda. We do not have to patiently listen while someone "weighs in" on our lives because we have the option of whether to give audience or not to this conversation. Jessie can make excuses to leave, set boundaries with Linda by telling her this is a private matter, and so on. In fact, Jessie does not have to explain her life to strangers or anyone else for that matter. Just because people ask us questions, does not mean we have to answer them.

Stand In Your Story Of Who You Are

We are much like authors of our own lives with several chapters at different points in time. While we make decisions along the way, we are determining our life story. We could just as easily be considered as artists as well who are filling up a blank canvas through our adventures and all the actions we decide to take. So in these different installments or "chapters" (seasons) of your life or as you are the artist filling up your canvas, who are you? What is the story you have about yourself? When you have a personal story about who you are through the different seasons of your life, you are able to stand with core confidence in the face of other challenging people who try put you in an ***emotional box of their understanding***. When someone says: "I know you and who you really are", you do not have to go into their "emotional box" (their version of reality or truth) in order to gain their approval. Instead, you can depend on your own story and know to your core who you really are in life. You have been in situations like this before and you know how you acted. Remember you know yourself better than anyone because you live inside of yourself every day. Just like when I was dumped by the older man earlier in my twenties who told me I am boring, I can rely on my story of myself through the seasons as I recall all my adventures and who I am. I give him permission to "not see me" and I give myself permission to not destabilize, second-guess myself, and "place myself in the emotional box of his understanding." In my truth I am not a boring person and it is my version of reality that matters most in this world.

The Name And The Shame

If loved ones close to us have done something through their "acting-out", addiction, or unhealthy behaviours we may feel embarrassed as well as humiliated particularly if we feel like these actions have reflected on us by association. When we are out in public, we may "put on a coat of shame" of personal humiliation in that we feel like people are watching us with their judgments. The challenge is to not "wear the name" around judgements that people may or may not have of us and to not "carry the shame." Sometimes we are our own worst enemies when we react to hypothetical scenarios around what we believe others are thinking of us. When we have a consistent story of who we are according to the various seasons we have lived in life so far, then we gain the perspective to rise above our circumstances. In fact, we do not give other people the power to determine our value or worth. There are individuals in life who like to serve as "emotional vampires" in that they feel energized or "feed off of" the negativity, upsets, or dramas of others in life. When we destabilize and allow ourselves to feel shame as we worry about the judgments of other gossiping people or "emotional vampires", then we are not only giving our power away, but we are also serving ourselves up for the feeding of others. We have a choice to stand in our emotional core and in spite of the gossip or unhealthy behaviours of others, we can stay strong in who we are as we live our own personal truth. This means that we do not live for the approval of others and we do not have to give audience or attention to those who are preparing for us to fall so that they can gain pleasure from our discomfort.

Who Are You Through The Seasons?

Have you ever tried to really get to know yourself? This may seem like a silly question, but if you have lived a life so far whereby you are overly-concerned about the judgments as well as opinions of others then you may have a habit of "shutting down parts of who you are" as you conform to the ideas of what other individuals think. Therefore along the way, you stopped yourself from truly getting to know yourself at deeper levels. We have seasons of our life and with insight we gain knowledge around who we are, what we like, and what we dislike as we identify our own idiosyncrasies. What if you had the ability to re-invent yourself into your fullest potential without limitation? Who would you be and what would you be doing? This is your story and your life. When you stand solid in a strong sense of who you are, you cannot be destabilized by other people's versions, truths, or opinions of your potential.

Gaining Perspective

One of the reasons why we give others so much power is because we begin second-guessing ourselves when we encounter others with confidence who have no qualms about telling us who we really are or how we should think in life. Out of our needs for others' approval, we can easily lose perspective around who we really are or our personal story of ourselves through the seasons. The personal story we have around who we are and our potential for our lives is critical. It is with this personal positive story that we feel energized to maneuver through the emotional boulders as well as challenges of our lives. Just like the "little engine that could" train in the children's story we can go up emotional mountains and through obstacles with our internal self-talk saying to ourselves "I know I can...I know I can..." When we have a personal story of confidence around our abilities (which have been tested previously through different seasons), we tap into that confidence because we know we have been in this place before in life and we can succeed again. Even if we don't feel confident at the moment and have failed in the past, there is valuable learning along the way and we can take the lessons from those experiences because we are more equipped to deal with what is happening in our lives now.

An Ugly Moment In Time

There will be times in life also whereby we may feel like we are hitting an emotional wall or that things in this world are out of control. This could be a time of tremendous suffering as well as an opportunity for incredible personal growth. When we connect with our personal story of who we are through the different seasons, then we remember our potential. The challenge of the moment does not seem insurmountable despite the suffering we may feel at the time. This may be an "ugly time" in life, but this is not my life. We have the choice of whether to let an ugly moment in time define the rest of our lives. My story of who I am is independent of what is happening right now or what the world is reflecting back to me about myself. I know myself through the seasons of my life and there have been some very cold winters along the way. Definitely, I will not freeze to death because I have learned how to protect myself from the elements. When we tap into our story of ourselves through the seasons of life, we gain proper perspective and realize that we do not have to destabilize or "go under" with the challenges we are confronting today. With every situation there is a reason as we get to see the unfolding of God's larger story for our lives and His greater will. He is molding us as well as shaping our characters in preparation for our next chapter or installment of our life through the seasons. Also from every Winter there is a Spring and then a Summer. Some Winters just feel longer than others during particular years.

Dimension Three: Filling Yourself Up

My understanding of what energizes me and brings me joy as I focus on my dreams, goals, and passions in life.

We live in a society that loves to promote an external sense of happiness. Buy this car, get the latest techno gadget, decorate your house this way, use this brand of detergent and your life will be happy in an instant way. Movies also promote this romantic ideal like the movie "Jerry Maguire" (with Tom Cruise) that one day we will meet our other half who will "complete us." The process of "meeting another half" or a life partner is wonderful but they cannot be the source of happiness. That great life partner also has gas, likely leaves socks on the floor, and may not even put their dishes away properly. The challenge is to become responsible for our own happiness independent of what is happening in the outside world. Within us, we can create our own sense of serenity or contentment. If a partner brings us a coffee in the morning, this is wonderful and a delightful surprise but they are not our source of happiness. This means we enjoy people and they tremendously enhance our lives, but we can stand strong within ourselves with inner contentment.

If we place our sense of happiness outside of ourselves then we will live in an emotional state that is much like a rollercoaster. This means that we can only be happy when "all is well in our worlds" which if you are like most people and you want moments where everything lines up perfectly according to your expectations then this may happen about four times in life. Something will always "be off" or not quite right. Even if you are celebrating a massive victory, chances are that someone somewhere in your emotional world is going through a bad time so if your sense of happiness is outside of you then you may feel obligated to hold yourself back from even rejoicing in the face of tremendous blessings because others are not doing well. If your sense of happiness comes from others and how they are treating you, then the attention they give you will never be enough because you will expect them to fill up the "emptiness" inside of you. Nobody can heal the holes in our hearts and make us feel so full of love that we are buoyed up and ready for each day. If they do, then they hold a tremendous responsibility as serving as active cheerleaders for our lives. Such people must be exhausted and we may still feel like all the love they are giving us is not enough for our own satisfaction.

When we make the shift to realizing that we are responsible for our own happiness we are able to experience a sense of freedom. A sense of contentment must come from within ourselves regardless of what is happening in our outside worlds and it is independent of the levels of active love and attention we are receiving from others. This means we learn that we can be okay no matter what! We can give up trying to control the outcomes of situations because we only have to manage ourselves. With this insight we can lighten our loads. We are not responsible for other people's feelings because they "choose" their emotions, and we can love them as well as be kind, but we do not expect them to be responsible for our happiness. Instead, our happiness comes from within ourselves.

What is your source of joy? What makes you happy? What energizes you and makes you feel alive? What gives you hope? Many people have parts of themselves that are shut-down especially if they have served as people-pleasers trying to gain the approval of others. Now as you look at the potential of your life, you get to examine what makes you happy.

As an author or artist of your own life, what sources of joy are you going to write into your chapters in life or place in your blank canvas of art?

Your Personal Inventory

Many people feel initially overwhelmed at the prospect of having to identify sources of joy in their worlds. As people, we can easily acclimatize to negativity and become victims in life feeling like others are "doing things to us." We may have even placed our source of personal power on to others by believing that if these individuals will "get it" by figuring out that what they are doing is wrong then we can finally be happy. With such a process, we are "wishing our lives away" and letting the valve of life happiness slowly drain away like a balloon losing air.

If you step into your greatest potential, then you have a chance to grab back the "reins" of your own life by becoming responsible for your own happiness. One way to explore your sources of joy in life is to do a personal inventory by listing all of the energy drains as well as energy rejuvenators in your world.

Exercise:

Write down all the people, places, situations, things, and activities that drain you. What do you dread? What absolutely "sucks the life out of you?" What are you experiencing and how do you know you are drained? Be careful of becoming resentful around all the ways people "should" not be doing what they are doing and so on. You are solely responsible for your own happiness.

Now write down all the people, places, situations, things, and activities that energize you. What do you look forward to? What are you doing so that you feel that sense of being "in the zone", in joy, or time passes quickly? What fills your soul and makes you feel alive?

Then look at your life. Have you filled up your world with obligations, "time sucks", and energy drains? Do you ever engage in an activity for an hour and think: "Wow this is an hour of my life I will never get back again?" Do you have a conversation with someone and hope to some degree that the earth would just open up and suck you into the ground so that you would have relief for even an instant even though you would technically be suffocating in the dirt. Your thought may be that such torture would be more pleasurable than talking to this person? I have a question for you....why are you putting yourself through this pain?

Now look at the balance of energy drains and energy rejuvenators in your life. If you are responsible for your happiness, then there may need to be some obvious emotional housecleaning that can go on in your life. It is up to you to take your personal inventory and start eliminating or reducing the amounts of energy drains while "building in" the energy rejuvenators.

Feeling Selfish

When many people begin the process of "filling themselves" up with energy rejuvenators and sources of joy, they feel guilty like they are being selfish by taking time away from their children, spouses, and so forth. Some culturally conditioned women believe that they are now being a bad spouse by taking care of themselves. The reality, is that if we do not reclaim back the "me" in the "we" of our relationships, then we do not have a life. We are emotionally burning-out and becoming a shadow of ourselves as we disregard our own personal needs. Consider the oxygen mask protocol within airplanes. When an airplane hits turbulence and the oxygen masks fall down, the protocol is to put the mask on yourself first so that you can breathe. If you cannot breathe, then you are of no good to anyone else. Now the mother who is sitting beside her child may feel like she should put the oxygen mask on her child first, but what if she passes out in the process? Both her and her child are in trouble.

With people-pleasing patterns, we are all too willing to take care of everyone else's needs out of our desires for their approval while completely disregarding ourselves. Many individuals are "running on emotional fumes" in their lives on the verge of "burning out" their engines. Such people have not taken the time to "fill their emotional gas tanks" along the way with energy rejuvenators or sources of joy.

The reality is that we are more engaged, emotionally-available, as well as intentional around the needs of others when we have taken the time to "fill ourselves" up with energy rejuvenators. In fact, when we fill ourselves up first we have more to give of ourselves to others. We become better business owners, employees, spouses, parents, friends, and so forth because we are not overwhelmed. Our quality of interactions with others significantly improves when we have excess energy by "filling ourselves up" first.

Manage The Busy Monster In Your Life

Many people are crisis-driven and they are responding in a "knee-jerk" reaction to the issues in their lives. Such individuals are "on the go" and are ping-ponging off of people, places, and things as they rush around trying to get things done. If we are not careful, the monster of busyness can completely overshadow our lives. As a result, we do not grow into our potential because much like walking through "emotional molasses" we are just trying to manage the overwhelm or even sludge in our lives. Everything requires effort and if we do not engage in self-care or take time out to have "me-time" by participating in our sources of joy then we will continue to rush around everywhere physically while not getting anywhere emotionally. Instead, we will be running on the "emotional treadmill" of our lives furiously with the end result being that the track will spin faster without our ability to keep up and then we have the inevitable "face plant" (fall) as we slip off the tracks in overwhelm.

Golf Balls And Sand

Imagine that you can take a vacation once all of your work is completed. If you are like many people you can work twenty-four hours a day, seven days a week, and still not get all of your work done. If you are running on the emotional treadmill of life there will not be a time when life will settle down and you can finally take a vacation or participate in sources of joy in your life. Instead, you have the option of becoming a "steward of your own joy" and you have to manage as well as protect it with all of your might or power. People along with the demands of life are all too willing to "steal our joy" and dump their responsibilities as well as expectations on our heads.

Pretend you have a jar, a pile of golf balls, and sand. The sand represents the busyness of life and the golf balls are healthy habits, "me-time", vacations, and so forth. Now if you pour the sand into the jar you will not be able to jam the golf balls into that same jar. The sand will have taken up all of the space. But if you put the golf balls in the jar first then you can pour the sand around the golf balls and fit this all in the sand. This metaphor is much like taking a vacation or enjoying your healthy habits that bring you joy. If you block-out your calendar or schedule your moments to experience joy, then busyness will never overshadow your happiness.

In many ways we have to become "rigorous protectors" or stewards over our own joy or we will let stress, anxiety, and fear take hold of the center of our lives as we become consumed in negativity. We cannot move into the potential of our lives if we are weighed down by such negative emotions which will erode our confidence. The challenge is to notice what makes us happy, to "reclaim our happy", and then to furiously "protect our happy" from others who are all too prepared to try and take it away from us. We can "renew" as well as energize our sense of happiness by flooding our worlds with sources of joy. For every challenge or task that is draining, make sure you have adequate sources of joy at your disposal. With conscious intentional thought we may even need to organize moments that bring us joy or happiness rather than waiting for happiness to "show up" in our lives. Blessings are wonderful and glory goes to God for creating these opportunities. Then there are the regular small things in life that bring us joy. We can actively stack up those sources of joy into our daily life so that we can immerse ourselves in joy each and every day if even only for a few minutes as a way to re-energize. Often we know what it is we need to do and it is just a matter of giving ourselves permission to do so while also creating the necessary time. Joy needs to be a top priority in our worlds!

Your North Star

Every day we have a choice around where to concentrate our energies. What will we do? What will get done? What are our priorities? If we develop larger passions, goals, as well as dreams then we have a sight line of where we are wanting to be in the future. As the emotional storms of life (problems) "blow in" and we are off course, one way of getting back on track is to focus on our emotional north star for direction. Our north star is the "why" of change and what we are moving toward. What is your goal of the future? This way you can become more energized as you take one more step closer towards fulfilling your potential.

Dimension Four: Expression Of Self

How I am able to express myself and create my mark on my surroundings or environment.

When we start to stand strongly in the core of who we are, we build a life from the inside out. Everything around us flows from our core values and our sense of selves. In other words, our "outsides match our insides." The blessings we experience in our outside worlds match with the self-esteem we feel on the inside of ourselves. When we have a sense of value that flows from the inside out we can allow ourselves to feel self-worth and compliments from others, blessings in life, and all the good things in this world feel comfortable as well as attainable. We step into our value and embrace all that is wonderful rather than feeling like an imposter or unworthy of good things. Now we have the opportunity to not only connect in our value, but also express ourselves.

As people we have an emotional legacy or a spiritual imprint of how we impact the lives of others around us. We bring with us an energy and as we talk with others or share time with them, we impact these people in particular ways. What is your emotional mark on the world?

Also we have a physical mark on our environments as we find ways to express ourselves. Our homes serve as our sanctuaries, so how can you express yourself in your environment through decorating your surroundings? As you cook, how are you filling the air with an aroma? In your core, you have a presence and everything flows from the inside out into a form of expression. Our challenge is to come up with innovative ways of self-expression whether it be through decorating our environments, enjoying art, or being creative in some way.

Flow is the sense of transcendence we achieve when we reach out and connect to something greater than ourselves. As people we achieve "flow" or we "go into the zone" when we immerse ourselves into self-expression. As a result, we can create a tremendous sense of joy, contentment, or even intense satisfaction by serving as creators as we invent things and find ways of expressing ourselves. Such moments are even more satisfying when we can give the glory to God and praise the Lord in the process. Furthermore, these moments are wonderful when shared in community. This way we transcend ourselves and reach out to a larger community by contributing our own "offerings" as we find ways to achieve self-expression for the larger good of others. There is a lot of satisfaction we can experience when we create something that can be offered to others while we express ourselves and also give to a larger community at the same time. For many people music, cooking, or even crafts are forms of self-expression that can also be shared in community.

We enhance our core confidence when we have "offerings" of ourselves that flow from the inside out. By reaching out and connecting to something outside of ourselves and with self-expression we are in the creative flow of life. With this process we enhance our personal value, feel like we have something to contribute, and we are creative as well. The result is that when we feel like we have much to offer and we are able to express ourselves, we achieve stronger self-confidence as we grow into our greater potential.

Dimension Five: Spiritual Connection

How God utilizes me and my gifts as I have a sense of giving back.

Romans 12:4-7

"For just as each of us has one body with many members, and these members do not all have the same function, so in Christ we, though many, form one body, and each member belongs to all the others. We have different gifts, according to the grace given to each of us. If your gift is prophesying, then prophesy in accordance with your faith; if it is serving, then serve; if it is teaching, then teach; if it is to encourage, then give encouragement; if it is giving, then give generously; if it is to lead, do it diligently; if it is to show mercy, do it cheerfully."

We all have spiritual gifts from God given to us by Him in order to carry out His higher purpose for our lives. The challenge we have is to be in conscious contact with God so that He can direct us towards how to grow those gifts as well as give back to others. This way we can glorify God. We serve God by utilizing our gifts for His purpose and by loving others along the way.

As Christians it may seem obvious that we need to maintain an active spiritual connection to God. The difficulty, however, is that God can easily become absent from our thinking as we connect to a fallen world that teaches us we need to only depend on ourselves and that powerful people just "take charge" and "make it happen." With self-will we build our lives and forget to keep God at the center of our worlds. Also some people are in a spiritual crisis in which they are "mad at God" because they are unhappy with their suffering, current problems, or other challenges in life. They feel like God is "picking on them" or even worse that God does not care and that He has "turned His back" on them. Christians live by faith and even in the midst of situations we do not understand, the challenge is to still draw closer to God and to step into His larger story of what is happening.

The Lord is our source of strength in this world. In Psalm 3:3 we learn how the Lord is our shield and it is Him who *lifts up our heads*. When we are in conscious connection with God by drawing to Him for strength, then the Lord infuses us with grace which reaches down through our emotional core so that we feel that core lovability, we know who we are through the seasons of life, we fill ourselves up with sources of joy and God is in all of those activities, we express ourselves and share the glory of the Lord, as well as maintain constant contact with Him. Our spirits become full from the inside out and we do not experience a sense of emotional emptiness or a "void" within ourselves. Instead, we are complete, in the light, actively connected with God, and walking out His higher purpose in this world. We operate out of our core and the Lord infuses this core with His grace as well as strength. This way, we can be equipped for anything in life as we grow into our greatest potential. We become worthy of the calling God has for us in this world.

Operating Out Of Your Emotional Core

The goal is to wake up each day equipped to deal with whatever challenges and while "living life on life's terms" we are okay no matter what. If we go into a negative thought spiral, we notice it, pull ourselves back and work on ways to strengthen as well as operate out of our emotional core. Out of our emotional cores, we are able to connect with our feelings, have a voice, and raise our personal value. This means that we can express our thoughts as well as our needs in our relationships. With a sense of self independent of others and what is happening in the world, we can protect as well as operate out of our emotional cores as we renew our sense of inner confidence. With internal strength we no longer let fear as well as negativity overshadow our lives and we can live in freedom.

As I feel strong inside, I give myself permission to be me. Out of this freedom, I then give you permission to be you. I stop trying to manage as well as control things in life because I know with certainty that whatever happens I can definitely handle it. This does not mean bad things won't happen or that I won't be shaken. But I have the core resiliency and emotional fitness to deal with whatever comes along. I no longer shut down parts of myself for approval. Instead, I allow others to have their "emotional processes" (feelings as well as personal truth) and I can let them work through their issues as I detach in a loving and healthy way with compassion. I know I have my own emotional housecleaning to do so I stay focused on my area of control which is related to myself as well as my reactions to people or situations. As a result, I draw closer to God and keep growing as I surrender old parts of myself that I need to die unto which are no longer serving me or my life very well.

The Doorway Of Respect

As I develop core confidence by strengthening my emotional core, my life becomes less complicated. I am no longer prepared to tolerate poor behaviour from people. In effect, I have taught people how to treat me and if people want to be in my life then they need to meet me in my value by treating me with respect as well as kindness. I will not tolerate anything less and in return I try to be the best person I can be by living according to God's kingdom principles in my relationships. This means I try to be slow to anger (James 1:19) and I am careful of the words I say as I focus on building up others (Romans 14:19) rather than tearing them down with my words or actions. Effectively, I have built a door of respect and people who enter my life will not be allowed in unless they meet me in my value and with respect. I will not compromise my values or self by "accepting their invitations to roll around in the mud" through gossip, negativity, drama, or other spiritually immature behaviours. Instead, I take my relationships as well as interactions with others to higher healthier ground and I use my voice to communicate my needs as well as feelings. With your relationships being less complicated you have more room for your calling in life so that you can live in core confidence carrying out God's will rather than constantly tripping in other people's drama along your path of life.

Chapter 5

Don't Jump Into Swimming Pools Without Water!

Now we have learned about how to develop strong self-confidence by activating our emotional cores. As a result, with emotional fitness we can "power up" for anything in life and feel the ongoing strength to deal with all kinds of challenges while also having the inner resiliency to develop as well as accomplish our goals. We have found within ourselves an energy battery or a way to "power up" that can keep us going. While learning the five dimensions of the LIFES, we have explored the necessity of having God at the center of your life. We are able to build up these five dimensions of core confidence with the infusion of God's grace as well as strength. What we want to be careful of, however, is feeling all "powered up", ready to take on the world as we then start driving over emotional cliffs. We must have a sense of spiritual discernment to ensure that we are in God's will and carrying out His higher purposes. Furthermore, we do not want to be pursuing our goals to find out that we are way off track on some type of tangent and that God is not even in the plans we are carrying out at the moment. In our excitement, we may have forgotten to check if our plans are even in God's will. This mistake is very much like the metaphor of jumping into swimming pools without water. If we dive in head-first into a swimming pool without water it really hurts to smash our heads on the concrete. Then we may find out later that God was not even in these plans and instead we were powered by self-will on some type of tangent. This is a painful experience!

Blind Confidence

We can easily become excited about new ideas and then as we activate our emotional core along the five dimensions, we will begin feeling stronger core confidence like we have the abilities to carry out these plans forming in our minds. What we want to be careful of is feeling all "fired-up" as we then enter into situations blindly with confidence.

Some ways we have *blind confidence* include:

1) Assuming that if we think something and come up with a new idea that it is inspired by God and within the Lord's will.

2) Not checking our motivations and seeing potential dollar signs in terms of income in a new endeavour so we are prepared to make all kinds of large decisions because we just assume that with God's provision He will provide the abundance of money later. He may provide that money, but we have to check that this is within His will first without making assumptions.

3) Seeing in people what we want to see and not taking these issues into prayer. For example, "wearing rose-coloured glasses" and assuming the best in people without asking God for confirmation that we should even be working with such individuals on projects or entering into relationships with them.

4) Assuming that we live in an "invincibility bubble" and that bad things will not happen to us because we are Christians and are somehow protected by the Lord at all times. Therefore we believe we do not have to check in with the Lord's will because we have the ability to know for ourselves what God wants because "it feels right" or we are excited.

5) We focus on the vision of "what could be" without looking at the "reality of what is" and do not depend on God to help us navigate through the upfront hard work necessary to accomplish our goals. We want the end-result without the work and we underestimate our challenges because we are not in prayer with God gaining the Lord's assistance through preparing for problems or issues that will inevitably come along.

We Need Brakes!

When we are functioning on the power engine of self-will, then we are all "powered up" with gas and we do not look at the necessity of having brakes. If we drive without brakes then we will race around sharp turns in life with full confidence thinking that we know what we are doing as we then drive over emotional cliffs. In a deep walk with God in life, we need to be able to have the Lord serve as the brakes for us. God unfolds His vision for us in little pieces that we can handle or understand at the time. The Lord does not give us the entire picture of where we are going because He is preparing us where He is leading us in life. We may not yet be the people we are meant to be in the future carrying out His calling because we have old parts of ourselves like people-pleasing, lack of boundaries, eself-pride, and so forth that need to be tempered, refined, or emotionally-burned away. Essentially, on some level there are parts of ourselves holding us back and we need to die unto our old selves. Therefore God will send us "preparatory" learning lessons along the way in order to prepare us for the responsibilities or opportunities He will give us later. In many ways, these situations are tests of our character. If we pass them, then we are given more responsibilities or we get to see a little more of the "bigger picture" or unfolding story He has planned for us.

We know from Ecclesiastes 3:11 that God makes everything beautiful in it's time. So we can power ourselves up with core confidence, but God may be providing some brakes as He lines up details or situations in life. Therefore we may pray to God and He may put on the brakes around our requests by saying: "No", "Not now", or "Not this way." As we pray, we may be confident that what we are praying about is bound to happen according to our understanding at the time and that we are kind of stating the obvious but out of respect for God we are placing these issues into prayer. With such self-pride, we may not realize that we are so off-course with our understanding or that we need a learning lesson first. Also we may receive what it is that we want but have to be prepared that it will be in "God's way" and within "God's timing." I prayed at the age of 14 to marry my husband when I was 21 years old. The reality is that I was an emotional mess and so was my husband in those earlier years. We could not have appreciated each other or grown into who we are in our marriage now if we had not had some "hard-knocks" or preparatory life lessons before marrying each other thirteen years later. Also I thank God for many unanswered prayers along the way because if He had answered all of my silly requests, I would have been completely off-track for even being available to marry my husband in the first place.

Having A God-Led Life

As Christians, there is no doubt we have God in our hearts, but do we have the Lord at the center of our lives always as we walk out daily life? Or does God become absent from our thinking as we fall further into the trap or ensnarement of self-will? With self-sufficiency, we think we can manage our lives because we just have to work hard to accomplish our goals. In such a mindset, we think we are giving God a break because after all He is so busy we wonder why He would even care about someone as insignificant as us? A client said to me once: "Well, I don't really want to bother God with my silly prayers. The Lord is helping people with real problems like with all the hunger in the world." God has omnipresence as well as omnipotence so in His tremendous power to create and maintain the world, we are not inconveniencing the Lord with an active relationship with Him. God wants to be in a close relationship with his children (1John 3:1). Furthermore, we cannot accomplish anything without God. We are reminded in John 15:5 "I am the vine; you are the branches. If you remain in me and I in you, you will bear much fruit; apart from me you can do nothing."

The opportunity is to have a God-led life. In John 10, we learn about the value of allowing God to be the Shepherd of our lives.

John 10: 7-18

"Therefore Jesus said again, 'Very truly I tell you, I am the gate for the sheep. All who have come before me are thieves and robbers, but the sheep have not listened to them. I am the gate; whoever enters through me will be saved. They will come in and go out, and find pasture. The thief comes only to steal and kill and destroy; I have come that they may have life, and have it to the full. 'I am the good shepherd. The good shepherd lays down his life for the sheep. The hired hand is not the shepherd and does not own the sheep. So when he sees the wolf coming, he abandons the sheep and runs away. Then the wolf attacks the flock and scatters it. The man runs away because he is a hired hand and cares nothing for the sheep. 'I am the good shepherd; I know my sheep and my sheep know me—just as the Father knows me and I know the Father—and I lay down my life for the sheep. I have other sheep that are not of this sheep pen. I must bring them also. They too will listen to my voice, and there shall be one flock and one shepherd. The reason my Father loves me is that I lay down my life—only to take it up again. No one takes it from me, but I lay it down of my own accord. I have authority to lay it down and authority to take it up again. This command I received from my Father.'"

As fallible human beings with the potential of being lost in a fallen world with all kinds of cliffs, traps, as well as emotional snares we need a Shepherd in life. There will inevitably be "wolves" in our lives and without the Shepherd we can be stolen from as well as destroyed on many levels. Also God has our best interests in mind and He wants us to *have a life and live it to the full.*

Entrepreneurial Seizures

In the business book *The E-Myth Revisited*, Michael E Gerber describes the concept of an "entrepreneurial seizure" which is the point in which people develop a vision of their small business and become excited about the possibility of being their own bosses. Such a "seizure" happens when individuals examine the potential profit margins of what they could possibly earn in their new small business and with great gusto they charge forward to put all of these plans in place by investing without putting proper thought or safeguards in place. Even worse, many business owners think in the midst of an "entrepreneurial seizure" that they can just open a business, hire staff, and that the place will run itself. That is why so many businesses foreclose in the first year with business owners feeling disillusioned as well as bankrupted.

This concept of an "entrepreneurial seizure" is also important on a spiritual level. We are sheep and we need God as our Shepherd. If we do not have the Lord as our Shepherd in life, then we will get these "brain waves" or entrepreneurial seizures and consult with other "sheep" (people) who agree with us. Together we will charge around our pastures looking at potential profit margins for our new businesses or whatever next great idea occurs as we "bah" at each other and reinforce each other in the stupidity of our decisions. We think we are very smart when really we are charging over an emotional cliff towards a very painful fall. We need a Shepherd to guide us in life.

One of the most misinterpreted messages is from the movie "Field Of Dreams" starring Kevin Costner where he has a dream of building a baseball field in the middle of nowhere. One of our great Hollywood sayings comes from that movie which is "build it and they will come." Just step into faith. But what if you are powered by self-will and not acting in God's plans at all? What if your plans are not according to God's will and you "build it" and "they do not come?"

I have had many entrepreneurial seizures in my time as I explored all kinds of projects such as event planning, setting up learning centers, pet advertising, building up funeral services with grief counselling, and so on. There are no limits to my imagination. The problem is that my ability to "go off-track" is epic. I remember sitting in a large store-front space locked into a lease that I was trying desperately to get out of while watching dollars slip down the drain crying out to God wondering how such a "great idea" could have had such devastating effects? Two days before my lease expired, with all of my credit cards at a maxed out level, barely able to keep my financial head above water, I sat in the empty storefront sobbing. The new lease holder had "broken in" the night before as he had obtained a key early and had tossed some of my belongings to the side. The open area was now covered in pink chalk lines showing the renovation plans he was going to make as he took over the space. The pink chalk lines looked like "pens" or square cages whereby new walls would be built and so forth. I pulled my bible out and began praying. I opened up my bible to John 10 and read about God as my Shepherd. During that time, my tears turned to giggles at the irony of the pink chalk drawings over the walls and floors. I accepted that I was an "entrepreneurial sheep" and this was my pen as I called out to my Shepherd. It was at that moment my self-pride broke a little and I realized that my "great ideas" always needed to be within God's will and at every point in turn with conscious contact with the Lord that I needed to check-in. I was fully prepared to hear the words "No", "Not now", or "Not this way" in my life and with these great words I could avoid being locked into very expensive leases while being really off-track in life. I had jumped head first into a swimming pool with no water and vowed not to smack my head on concrete again. It hurts!

The empty swimming pools in your life may be business ventures , investments, new relationships, home renovations, or whatever "new ideas" you come up with. I see advertising for Christian single on-line dating sites and I shudder inside especially when the message is that God will find you the next love of your life or that there is some magical destiny that people happened to find each other on-line when really they have twelve or more "other magical people in profiles" that they are checking out at the same time. In that atmosphere there are all kinds of empty swimming pools to jump into with the great illusions we can have, believing that we have found our soul-mate, and then getting caught up in the "magic" of meeting someone new only to find out they are crazy! As we draw people quickly into the center of our lives we can just as easily discover who they really are and wonder how to get them out of our worlds just as fast.

Spiritual Discernment

The synchronicity of timing does not mean that this is a sign that we need to charge ahead into a swimming pool without water. I thought that the fact that the store-front lease was available was a "sign" that I needed to lock into a very expensive lease in which I could not get out of at all. Since someone else at the same time wanted this lease, I charged ahead without much thought and signed on the dotted line. In reality, we were both competing for the same swimming pool with no water and eager to be the first to dive in head first into the concrete. I had not allowed God to be my necessary Shepherd. Also in relationships, crazy people can show up unexpectedly in disguise and what appears as the "magic" of timing is really a set-up. Furthermore, appliances and home renovation materials will "go on sale" and it is not necessarily a "sign" that we need to spend thousands of dollars going ahead on our projects. We become vulnerable when we lock on to the end result of making lots of money, finding a great love, creating a home so new that people will be envious and so forth. Once we have that end-goal in mind we can easily power into self-will to make those outcomes happen while leaving God's will out of the mixture. There is always a fine line between confidence and complete stupidity.

With spiritual discernment, we check-in with God to ensure that we are not "off-track" and that we are operating in accordance with His will. If we are not in the Lord's will then we become prepared to "let go" of our plans having the faith that God will show us the larger picture of what He has in mind for us to do at the next step.

How Can We Get Confirmation?

Some people will "lay the fleece" or wait for a sign around confirmation of their plans. The concept of the fleece comes from

Judges 6: 36-40, in which Gideon dictated the sign of confirmation by putting out the fleece and if the fleece was dry while the ground was wet with dew then it was a *sign* that Israel would be his in victory. This is controversial in that some people would argue that it is with self-pride and arrogance that Gideon is "dictating" or determining how the conformation of God should occur. In my opinion, people need to be careful around "organizing signs" or putting God through tests particularly around a yes/no answer especially if they are attached to an outcome of a particular action. For example, Cynthia wonders if Leonard "is the one" or her future husband? She is excited that he may like her and ask her out on a date. Cynthia asks God for a "sign" and says if Leonard phones in the next fifteen minutes, then it is a "sign" that he is to be her future husband even though they have never even dated. Surprisingly Leonard does phone and Cynthia now has the expectation that she will end up through destiny marrying Leonard one day in the future and she thanks God for the "sign" only to feel completely disillusioned one month later as she is mad at God for letting her have faith in Leonard. He is a serial cheater and Cynthia was one of ten women he was dating who he took money from because he is a con artist. Of course Leonard called Cynthia and courted her because she had money and he wanted to invest in a new business. But Cynthia was so caught up in the illusion of "who" Leonard could be and she was lonely after just getting out of her own divorce that she was waiting for a new prince charming to come along and save her from her own life. Cynthia did not hold up the image of Leonard to God in prayer and she was not prepared to listen to the Lord saying "no" to this situation. In fact, if Cynthia was looking for "signs" she needed to open up her eyes to the fact that after she first met Leonard he asked her if she lived in one of those expensive homes on the hills and joked that he was looking for a "sugar mama." Without having the Lord as her shepherd, Cynthia did not realize she has had just let the wolf in the door.

Ways To Gain Confirmation

1) Realize that God does not always work in yes/no answers
When God is unfolding a vision to us around where He wants us to go as He shares with us His higher plans, along the way we are growing into who He wants us to be. Sometimes we can do things and such actions are inconsequential to God's larger plans so it doesn't matter whether "yes" we do something or "no" we do not do something. Therefore in conscious contact with the Lord, we can always just ask or keep inviting God into our lives.

2) Big decisions need to be bathed in prayer
When we are going to make big decisions around moving, signing storefront leases, participating in large scale home renovations, and so forth we need to "bathe" these projects in prayer by going to the bible and pulling out scriptures, writing these scriptures into a journal, talking to people for wise counsel so we see this project from many sides, and so forth. God speaks to us through people by lining up key messages. If most people are saying "no" and things are not working well then this may be a sign to not proceed at this time or to find out in prayer how to adjust our plans accordingly.

3) Doors open and close in our lives
If we are meant to be somewhere doing something according to God's will, then He will take us there. If we are to stop functioning on the power engine of self-will, and want to be the sailboat then it is with resistance that God fills our sails with wind to charter our course. This means that opposition or resistance may show up in our lives as a sign that we are

meant to be somewhere else. All of a sudden a job that has gone well for several years can turn into our greatest nightmare! If God wants to move you somewhere He may make it so uncomfortable for you in your current circumstances that you begin moving. When it was time for me to leave a job, it became very clear because I was often bored, uncomfortable, and no matter how hard I tried to fix things everything kept falling apart. The doors of that chapter were closing and new doors were opening up. With the resistance, negativity, or even opposition I had with "doors closing" I was pushed to move towards the "new doors opening up" as different opportunities started appearing on the horizon. God was using pain as well as discomfort to move me towards the next step in His plans for me.

4) God moves like the waves
God often speaks in a whisper. If we do not turn down the volume of noise of thoughts in our minds, we may not be able to hear him. This is why we do not lean on our understanding and instead draw close to God. As the Lord gains momentum, what were small messages or indications we should move in a particular direction become glaringly apparent. Then there are emotional waves that carry us to where we are meant to be as we often through pain as well as discomfort begin realizing that we need to go in another direction (God's will) unless we want to continue to be miserable.

5) God is not in a hurry
If we are making rash decisions based out of fear or worrying that someone will steal our chances and take something from us if we do not act fast, then we are not in God's will. If we are meant to be somewhere doing something, then God will clear the space for that to happen. The Lord is a perfect man-

ager of details as well as resources. If something is meant to occur, then the opportunity as well as resources will appear before you out of nowhere.

With core confidence we can "power-up" for anything in life and we develop the necessary strength or emotional fitness to carry out our goals as well as God's larger plans for us. Along the way, however, we have the opportunity to grow into a deeper relationship with the Lord so that we are not powered by self-will. The Lord is our Shepherd through life and with His guidance we can navigate that fine line of following his calling while also creating the necessary "soft landings" so that if we do make mistakes these decisions are not irreversible. With God by our sides and at the helm of our lives, we can "test the waters" but do not have to dive wholeheartedly into swimming pools that do not contain water. This way we can learn the lessons we need as God guides us through life without getting full scale concussions in the process.

Chapter 6
Jesus As Basecamp

Much of our journey through life is based on faith. We do not know what we are doing or where we are going a lot of the time. In particular, the plans we have for ourselves may be even larger or very different in God's will. In fact, we trust that He is in charge and that He is growing us into His greater purpose for our lives.

With 1 Corinthians 10:31 we are reminded "So whether you eat or drink or whatever you do, do it all for the glory of God." We build on our emotional core through the infusion of God's grace and there is a wisdom that we develop when we put God at the center of our lives. In our healing journeys, regular as well as intentional contact with God for our own strength is of the utmost importance. In Psalm 113:3, we are told "From the rising of the sun to the place where it sets, the name of the Lord is to be praised." As we maintain this conscious contact with God regularly throughout life and within our days we are infused with a yoke of grace from the Lord. We are protected as well as connected into an incredible strength that comes from God.

Mathew 11:28-30

"Come to me, all you who are weary and burdened, and I will give you rest. Take my yoke upon you and learn from me, for I am gentle and humble in heart, and you will find rest for your souls. For my yoke is easy and my burden is light."

God promises that in His "yoke" we will find rest in our souls and that this "burden is light."

As we navigate through our daily chores, errands, responsibilities, duties, as well as activities each day it is very easy to keep looking in the "mirror" of the fallen world and grow further from God. In fact, the Lord can become more and more absent from our thinking as we function in a world that pivots on key values such as self-sufficiency, instant gratification, focusing on accomplishments, embracing the value of status, and so forth. We can easily get spiritually lost as we build up more of our own self-will to tackle issues and utilize our minds to sort stuff out. Over time, we can even ask ourselves "Who even needs God?" When we fall on easy times, we might even think these blessings were created through our own hard work and efforts. Then when we fall on hard times, become bored, are frustrated and so forth we may find with our instant gratification-driven minds that we are drawn to outside things like chemicals, food, shopping, or other types of comfort to block out the pain. This way we create a "feel good" experience all on our own terms.

The difficulty of becoming spiritually lost is that we move further into spiritual unbalance and with self-sufficiency, self-absorption, as well as self-will we learn to "power our way" through situations to make them work out how we plan. We have a false illusion of being in control as we focus on managing outcomes of situations and trying to make things in our lives work according to our own way and within our own timing. If variables do not line up the way we want, then we force or manipulate circumstances to ensure they work according to our expectations. The "buy now and pay later" world of credit cards, credit lines, and reconsolidation loans is a perfect example of how with some fancy finagling we can get what we want, the way we want it, and now on our terms as we throw caution to the wind. Poof! Instant status and elevated standard of living which we may not even be able to afford but with faith in God we hope He will work it all out despite the fact that that we have pushed through on our own self-will without even consulting Him in the process.

As we progress further down the path of being spiritually lost, we keep "grasping" at what we want and have a sense of spiritual restlessness as we focus more on "powering our way through situations" and making things work according to our expectations. We end up projecting our will on to the world and then work hard to make things happen according to our expectations as well as image. In fact, we often surround ourselves with people who think like us and we believe we are part of an "us" who have it going on and understand how to get ahead as we work hard to manage outcomes as well as control variables in our lives. In a spiritually restless state we are drowning in the volume of noise of thoughts in our minds trying to figure out how to get ahead and make things work. With this focus on control on our own lives, we may lock into a death grip with issues trying to make it all work out according to how we want it to be. Can we save enough money to get that perfect house? Can I land that new job? Can we get our home interior to look the way we want? How do we get ahead? Can we get that newest techno gadget and by the way how did we ever exist without an I phone or a PVR? When we focus solely on what we want and how to set things up to make it happen, we become spiritually restless as well as dry. Our worlds become more and more about filling ourselves from the outside in with material items as well as goals rather than reaching out and connecting to the Higher Power outside of ourselves. God is placed on the backburner of our lives as an afterthought if we have time to think about Him as we charge on towards making what we want happen especially since we may live in the land of endless opportunities as well as possibilities.

In this intense self-willed state, we are not only spiritually restless but we become overwhelmed with trying to control everything, lining up things in our lives perfectly, and "making it all happen" towards what we want. Rather than taking cues from God around the direction we should go, we can feel fearful as we start to over-function even harder to make things work in our lives. As our minds spin and swirl in thought, the relief we seek needs to be a short blast and within a containable amount of time. Perhaps that relief exists within a bottle of sleep medication, some time on the internet surfing through social networking, going on shopping sprees, over-eating, or taking the edge off with alcohol, and so on. Escape and entertainment come in many different forms but when these outlets become our form of relief while we draw further away from God then we are in danger of becoming spiritually-dry. Our souls will not find rest in the fallen world and our spirits will thrash around in an unsettled state trying to fill an empty void with material things and acting-out behaviours that just make us that much hungrier.

As we trek out into the world and navigate around all kinds of traps and potential snares, we need a tour guide and a leader. We can still have those goals and enjoy a comfortable style of living, but we need an emotional as well as spiritual compass to know that we are heading in the right direction and not getting lost. Of course that compass is the Lord and we must regularly consult Him to check-in around whether we are getting off track in our lives.

Jesus As Your Basecamp

When we have a goal of climbing a high altitude mountain this is much like tackling any large goal or direction in life. In high altitude areas, we can easily develop altitude sickness, head out into life-threatening storms or weather conditions, and even have the possibility of death. We need a basecamp as a place to re-group and make very important decisions around whether to venture out or to wait for the storm to pass before we make our next move. Also when we set up basecamp we can climb the mountain and acclimatize to the air slowly by then coming back down to basecamp again to readjust. When we climb and then make steps back to basecamp, then we can slowly keep increasing our altitude in the climb while safely acclimatizing our bodies in the process.

Usually people set up a climbing regime such as 300-400m higher than the previous overnight accommodation. It is advisable to spend the day of altitude acclimatization doing a little trekking leading up to a short stay at a greater altitude before returning and staying overnight at the previous altitude. Therefore there is a need to set up a base camp. Now in a self-willed, ego-driven state people will charge up the mountain and want the status of having climbed "Everest" so that they can be a part of an elite few individuals in the world who have fulfilled this accomplishment. In self-will, people will disregard weather warnings and "power their way through situations" trying to climb as fast as they can while disregarding the acclimatization process. They will take unnecessary risks while claiming they have a superior athletic ability, an incredible climbing record of the past, and are not like most people with their higher than average lung capacity. This is why the path to Everest is marked with all kinds of make-shift tombstones as a memorial to the people who lost their lives on that mountain.

We can use this metaphor spiritually as we allow Jesus to become our basecamp. As we venture out into the fallen world each day we do so thoughtfully with prayer before we go and praying reflection once we return. All of our thoughts and plans are presented to the Lord as we allow Him to become the Shepherd of our lives. This lifestyle of having regular conscious contact with God and allowing ourselves to have a God-led life is critical and requires rigorous discipline. We must submit ourselves humbly before God each day and recognize with reverence God's power as well as understand the numerous ways we can get off track in our lives. Great decisions like maximizing our credit opportunities seem like good options at the time but now with the larger economy the way that it is in an "economic downturn" people in vast numbers are wondering how they could be dangling off of the edge of a cliff when that path seemed like such a great opportunity with a wonderful view at the time.

The need for Jesus as a basecamp is that much more critical when you are wanting to drown out pain with chemicals, shopping, food or other escapes or you are overwhelmed with fear as well as stress.

The Lord provides us with enduring strength to go out and face the world. We find our spiritual strength solely in Him.

John 4:13-14

"Everyone who drinks this water will be thirsty again, but those who drink the water I give them will never thirst. Indeed, the water I give them will become in them a spring of water welling up to eternal life."

Psalm 63:1 and 5-6; 7-8

1-"You, God are my God, earnestly I seek you; I thirst for you, my whole being longs for you, in a dry and parched land where there is no water." ; 5-6 " I will be fully satisfied as with the richest of foods; with singing lips my mouth will praise you. 7-8 "Because you are my help, I sing in the shadow of your wings. I cling to you; your right hand upholds me."

John 6:35

"Then Jesus declared, 'I am the bread of life. Whoever comes to me will never go hungry, and whoever believes in me will never be thirsty…"

John 6:47-51

"Very truly I tell you, whoever believes has eternal life. I am the bread of life. Your ancestors ate the manna in the wilderness, yet they died. But here is the bread that comes down from heaven, which people may eat and not die. I am the living bread that came down from heaven."

John 7:37-38

"'Let anyone who is thirsty come to me and drink. Whoever believes in me, as Scripture has said, rivers of living water will flow from within them. By this he meant the Spirit, whom those who believed in him were later to receive."

We find spiritual renewal in the Lord. With our minds we need to stay in contact and return after each day back to Jesus as our base camp.

Chapter 7
Your Higher Purpose In God's Story

In this journey, you have learned about the five dimensions of how to build up your emotional core as you develop core confidence as well as emotional resiliency. With Jesus as your base-camp and as the Shepherd of your life, you are now ready for anything! In fact, you are equipped with a tool box of skills through life. Then it happens...something so completely unexpected that it feels like all of the lights have gone out in your world. It is much like an emotional power failure and in this darkness you are groping your way along trying to grab on to objects that are recognizable so that you do not trip and fall. This emotional black-out or power failure may be related to an event that you did not anticipate happening as someone you care about breaks trust, a tragedy occurs, or something of major magnitude occurs in your life. As Christians, we are not necessarily protected from bad things happening in life. God does not waste a crisis and He will use such adversity in our lives to help us grow on deeper emotional as well as spiritual levels closer to His design of who we need to be in His plans for our lives. As we get older, chances increase significantly that there will be problems with our health, our parents will age as well as pass on which is a mathematical certainty because we are getting older, and then there is the possibility that bad things happen out of nowhere such as car accidents for example. Now you have a tool box of core confidence skills and emotional fitness for not only following your dreams and goals, but for managing all the "bad things" in life as well.

Managing Sagas

Sometimes in life we have problems in which the answers will not just occur to us overnight in prayer. People we love may not wake up one day and realize that they are making stupid decisions, there are lawsuits, people will fall ill for long periods, your parents may even develop Alzheimer's disease, and so on. There is no "quick fix" to such challenges. These major life challenges unfold in chapters and go on for a long time as they are kind of like a saga that appears to have no immediate end in sight.

These sagas are kind of like long dry valleys in our lives. During this time we may enter into a spiritual crisis because we are upset with God in that we think we have been faithful Christians only to find out that we are not "protected" from problems because we have a valley or a saga to endure. The challenge is much like Apostle Paul who says in 2Timothy 4:7-8: " I have fought the good fight, I have finished the race, I have kept the faith. Now there is in store for me the crown of righteousness, which the Lord, the righteous Judge, will award to me on that day—and not only to me, but also to all who have longed for his appearing." So how will you keep the faith in the face of extreme challenges in life? What will be your walk should you encounter a long dry valley?

The Journey Through Long Valleys

We learn about valleys in Psalm 23:

"The Lord is my shepherd, I lack nothing. He makes me lie down in green pastures, he leads me beside quiet waters, he refreshes my soul. He guides me along the right paths for his name's sake. Even though I walk through the darkest valley, I will fear no evil, for you are with me; your rod and your staff, they comfort me. You prepare a table before me in the presence of my enemies. You anoint my head with oil; my cup overflows. Surely your goodness and love will follow me all the days of my life, and I will dwell in the house of the Lord forever."

The ultimate valley of course is one of death. But there are many emotional valleys in life before that time comes. Our challenge is to develop a deeper walk with the Lord as he "refreshes" our souls. We lean on him and develop reverence which is a deep respect or awe as well as a loss of innocence because we know that challenges can happen. Our walk with God becomes more mature because we realize our smallness in this large world and that we are not in control. When we surrender with reverence we have a sense of awe for God and we allow the Lord to come back at His rightful place at the center of our worlds. In the face of sagas, we realize how insignificant and powerless we really are in life. As a result, God grows in His importance and we are able to retire our self-pride as we focus on His greatness. We are in pain, completely vulnerable, and totally exposed which we can only truly appreciate in the midst of walking a dry valley in our life where there appears to be no relief in sight. In the book of Jonah, we see Jonah who is writhing about on the sand after being spit up by the whale and how as people we are subject to the elements of our lives. Even Jonah learned that his dependence was not on material things for comfort like the gourd to provide him with shade from the oppressive heat, but rather that he needed to wholeheartedly surrender to the Lord. Similarly when faced with challenges, we can offer ourselves to the Lord completely in prayer for relief.

We also learn a lot about ourselves while walking through the valley because we are called to the strength of our core. It is often in the darkness that we find our greatest light. When we have a strong basis of an emotional core, we allow Jesus to serve as our basecamp, and we have respect/awe or complete reverence for God out of an awareness of our vulnerability. Then we can step into His calling or grow into the Lord's higher purpose for our lives. We become changed by the valley in our life in a positive way.

Tempered By The Valley

In order to move into the future of who we need to be in God's plans for our lives we have to be prepared to die unto ourselves and the Lord (out of His love for us) will put us through a process of "tempering" or "refining." Much like the silver that is tempered through fire and heat to be shaped as well as molded into it's higher purpose, we are "shaped" or "tempered" through affliction or our burdens.

In Psalm 66:10-12, we learn:

"For you, God, tested us; you refined us like silver. You brought us into prison and laid burdens on our backs. You let people ride over our heads; we went through fire and water, but you brought us to a place of abundance."

We feel the burning of the heat and the discomfort of being vulnerable to the elements and we become changed by this process while walking through the valley. Everything that seemed problematic before now appears superficial and it is in our greatest pain as well as suffering that we learn about compassion. The prideful, judgmental, as well as fearful parts of ourselves are "burned away" because it is through pain that we learn to rise to our greatest potential and connect with God for His strength.

I believe that it is through these valleys that we grow deeper in character and become prepared for growing into our worthiness of the Lord's calling and His plans for us. We are changed and are now ready for the responsibility of stewardship of His higher purposes. Once we are changed, we can be brought to a place of "abundance" because we have learned the necessary spiritual maturity to be able to handle these responsibilities.

A Harvest Of Righteousness

With all of our actions we "bear fruit" that reflects the value of our character. We can have rich relationships, a deep faith, and all of these qualities will show up as metaphorical "fruit." If we are alone and with anger have pushed everyone out of our lives then the "fruit" of our worlds will be "bitterness." As we learn huge lessons and our characters become transformed through valleys in our life, we have the ability to develop fruit as well as a harvest of righteousness.

Ezekiel 36:8-11

"'But you, mountains of Israel, will produce branches and fruit for my people Israel, for they will soon come home. I am concerned for you and will look on you with favor; you will be plowed and sown, and I will multiply the number of people living on you, even the whole house of Israel. The towns will be inhabited and the ruins rebuilt. I will increase the number of people and animals living on you, and they will be fruitful and become numerous. I will settle people on you as in the past and will make you prosper more than before. Then you will know that I am the Lord."

With our choices, actions, and decisions in life we impact others and this world around us. We will bear branches of fruit. If we become tempered through the challenges of our life we can bear amazing fruit by positively impacting others with our actions of righteousness. In order to get to this level of spiritual maturity, sometimes God accelerates this process of tempering us through our afflictions or burdens. God does not necessarily orchestrate the suffering in our lives but if through our free will or the free will of others troubles are created, God with His mercy may accelerate these conditions so the problems are over with more quickly. What appears to be an emotional train wreck of problems in life becomes worse before it becomes better. The troubles are accelerated and it is out of mercy that we can have closure but before we get to resolution, situations appear worse from our understanding or perspective. In essence, God can make good out of the bad we have created for ourselves or which others have done to us through deceitful actions. During crisis, it is as if a "flash fire" is running through the center of our lives and things appear to be out of control. But even with flash fires, there are advantages as well as opportunities. Farmers will often set their fields on fire before a harvest in order to "burn away the old weeds" and make way for the new, abundant harvest. The challenge in our lives is to detect a "flash fire" in our worlds and to not lean on our own understanding, but instead step into faith. The lessons from these problems are painful and will "burn", but the result is an abundance of harvest in our characters. We will be forever changed as a result of this process.

Now if we learn these valuable lessons we can avoid future problems as well because we will have the necessary "emotional rudders." Much like a ship that turns on a rudder so does our tongues steer the course of our lives by what we say (James 3:4-10). Our words are reflective of our character and with deeper life lessons we grow as well as change. As a result our words will change and we may be more prepared to "build people up" (1Thessalonians 5:11) as we walk out the Kingdom principles in our lives. With pain we grow and in our characters we take one more step towards righteousness as we watch the words we use.

So now as we walk forward we can be prepared with our strong emotional cores, core resiliency, as well as emotional fitness, Jesus as our basecamp, and reverence for God so that we are equipped to fulfill our dreams. Dr. Jerry Nance from the ministry Teen Challenge reminds us in his book *From Dream To Reality* that opposition and problems are part of life and we have to be prepared to take the lessons by using this learning for our own advantages along the way. Many people will share their stories of how they "failed their way to success." Therefore no one in life will ever be immune from challenges but if we are prepared to serve as the sailboat with God as our wind we can fill up our emotional cores with that resistance to charter a course beyond our greatest dreams. In the journey of life, we may not know exactly where we are heading with the Lord, but with a tool box of skills and emotional fitness around having the necessary core confidence while maturing in a deep relationship with God, we are ready for wherever that adventure takes us!

Chapter 8

Live The Choice Now!

I am going to give you a challenge that I will call the "One Year Place Challenge." Should you accept this mission, then you are committing to being in a better emotional place or healthiness in a year from now. This is much like drawing a start line through the center of your life as part of a "fresh start" or new beginning. What this means is that you are going to deal with an emotional issue in your life and finally put this problem to rest. Along your spiritual path you have encountered an emotional boulder which is a problem blocking your way to full happiness. You may feel like this boulder or obstruction is insurmountable and you can't possibly imagine how you are going to get over it, around it, and with the weight of this burden you most certainly cannot crawl under it. So there you are...stuck, defeated, fearful, and probably exhausted at the possibility of moving this boulder or problem out of your way.

The mystery that you do not know is that the emotional boulder before you is actually a pebble. What if you had the perspective to see your way around the boulder and had the energy to raise your leg high in the air to step over this obstacle? In fact, the issue is one of perspective so that you see the burdensome emotional boulder as the pebble that it actually is in this world. With emotional fitness, you have the energy, knowledge, and skills to "power up" for any challenge in your life. This means having the ability to reduce emotional boulders into pebbles in your world.

So let's begin this work! Your "One Year Place Challenge" begins right now! Three quarters of the work is identifying what you are even dealing with as an issue. Often we are reacting and feel like we are sliding out of control in our issues. By gaining perspective we figure out exactly what it is we are dealing with in the first place.

Step #1: Figure Out Why And How You "Lost Your Inner Happy."

This is the shadow of the emotional boulder or obstacle in your life. Your opportunity is to figure out exactly what is bugging you and why you are so unhappy right now? That natural joy within yourself is fading, hidden, or has been dampened like smothered coals in a furnace. What happened and how did you lose "your inner happy?" Yes, we have taken the word "happy" and turned it into a noun because it is a thing, an experience, a natural part of who you are living inside of you. God wants us to be happy and we know that the Lord wants us to live life to the fullest (John 10:10) and that He has plans to prosper us (Jeremiah 29:11). But, somewhere along the way you lost, gave away, or sold out your "happy" to someone else or a situation in your life.

Step #2: Identify The Thief

At this moment, your opportunity is to identify the thief or thieves (there may be more than one) that are stealing your "inner happy." This is the source of the shadow in your life. Why is the light of happiness and joy being overshadowed in your world? What is stealing your happiness? Chances are that you are allowing the thief of fear into your world and this thief is stealing, pillaging, and reeking havoc all over your inner emotional world!

So let's call out the two most common thieves into the light of God for healing.

Thief #1- "If Only Happiness"

We believe we can be happy "if only" someone else would change or do what it is that we expect them to do. If a situation would work out in a particular way, then we think we will be happy. Therefore with fear we try and manage outcomes and people in order to achieve certain results which we think will make us happy. What we do not realize is that happiness is not something outside of ourselves and is not dependent on what people are doing or how situations are working out in our lives. Instead, happiness is a state within ourselves that can be an ongoing peace in our connection with the Lord that is independent of what is occurring in our outer worlds. When we step into the covering of God's grace and connect to the Lord we trust that there is a larger story and we hand the details as well as burdens in our lives to God for healing. We stop, listen, and figure out His will of where we are going and what this all means right now!

Thief #2- "What If Overwhelm"

As people we live in two realities which includes the reality of what is happening right now and what we know for sure to be occurring. The other reality is the "what if", fear-based reality of "what could" happen in our worlds. Many of us as people are afraid to "let our guards down" and allow joy into our lives because we are worried that something bad will happen so we are prepared as we brace for another negative episode or anticipate how our greatest fears may come true. If we are ready, then we think the sting of such pain will not feel so bad when it arrives. Instead, with a negative state of mind we feel ready for the bad things to occur in our lives. If we are already anticipating disappointment, then when the disappointment arrives it won't be that bad...right? Or even worse some people delude themselves into believing that they are actually "warding off" bad things from happening as they play out their greatest fears in their minds. Such individuals believe that getting themselves "all worked up" is a way of averting bad things from happening. As a result, the "what if overwhelm" thief rushes in and takes charge of our inner worlds causing us to live in constant fear as well as anxiety!

So now you have the chance to identify the thieves of happiness in your emotional world. What is stealing your "inner happy?"

Congratulations! You have completed three quarters of the journey and a year is not even up! Maybe only a few minutes have gone by. Yes, it is that simple. Now you have gained back perspective. You are handing your happiness over to thieves who are creating chaos and a fear-based reality in your inner emotional world. When you step out of the fear, you see that the emotional boulder or obstacle in front of you is actually a pebble.

The challenge now is to maintain that perspective and this is a choice that you have a chance to live each day!

Step #3: Live The Choice Now!

You have the opportunity to "step into the worthiness" of happiness and joy in your life. This may sound strange but you actually have to give yourself permission to be happy or to reclaim back your life from fear and negativity. It is so much easier to be fearful, upset, and negative than to take the risk of being happy (letting your guard down) only to have something bad happen later. Therefore many people skip the process of allowing themselves to be happy because it is easier to just attach to all the bad stuff and get the pain over with in the meantime. Many individuals have an illusion of control if they work themselves into a state of fear or negativity. No one can make them feel bad because they have done it to themselves first!

How we feel comes from our thoughts. In fact our thoughts lead to our emotions which then result in our actions. If we want to change our reality, we must first address our thoughts and hold them up for examination. In fact, if we live a life whereby we are waiting for people to change or for situations to turn out in our favor, then we will be sadly disappointed. Our sense of "happy" will be outside of ourselves and we will live on an emotional rollercoaster of highs and lows rebounding off of situations, people, places, and things according to our expectations and our wills.

The opportunity is to "get our happy back" and "protect our happy" as we reclaim our lives back from negativity as well as fear. We allow people to have their own issues and their emotional process while focusing on ourselves and our healthiness. This means that we walk alongside people who are having issues but we allow them to "carry their own emotional backpacks" while becoming clear around our own "emotional back packs in life." As a result, we focus on our own issues and personal healthiness without collapsing under the weight of our own backpacks and those packs of everyone around us.

In the simplest terms, we make a commitment to be okay inside of ourselves even if things around us in our outer worlds are not okay at the moment. We do not pin our sense of happiness on externals (people/places/things outside of us.) Viktor Frankl in *Man's Search For Meaning* is a classic example of how as people one of our last human freedoms is where we place our minds. As a Psychiatrist trapped in Nazi concentration camps, Viktor Frankl showed us that we have a choice of how to think and that in spite of absolute human horror we have control over our thoughts around how to survive as well as maintain our inner emotional balance no matter what is occurring externally around us.

The problem is that many of us spiral in fear as well as negativity and we forget that we have a choice. In essence, we lose perspective and the pebbles in our worlds start becoming emotional boulders. We do not use our skills of emotional fitness and some of us may even distance ourselves from God in resentment because we feel that He is allowing bad things to happen to us.

In order to "live the choice now" we make the commitment to reclaim back our "inner happy." We remember that we have the choice and we actively keep the "thieves" at bay so that we do not hand over our inner peace to negativity.

The problem is that negativity and unhealthy or fear-based thinking builds up within our minds like a fog. We will call this the "fog of unhealthy thinking." When we are in the fog of fear, fog of addiction, or impaired thinking of any kind then we cannot see our way out of our situations. We forget we have a choice and we just continue on reacting in our old ways of doing things.

The challenge then is to "get out of our minds" and to get some perspective. This clarity comes with reaching out and connecting to something greater than ourselves. Furthermore, we are healthiest in community so when we take the time to connect with others through conversation, attend bible study groups, rigorously spend time alone with the Lord in devotion as well as prayer, and so forth then we create the emotional space as well as time to "get out of our heads" and into the light of God and His will. We stop panicking in fear and the volume of noise in our minds of thoughts slows down as we develop clarity around our direction or path according to God's larger design for our lives.

CPA Recovery System

One way of keeping the fog of unhealthy thinking at bay and to manage the motivation to "live the choice now" by staying healthy is to build a support system. This means:

a) Creating a positive action or a commitment to positive action (CPA). What will you do to stay emotionally healthy?

b) Take an on-line course to learn about why/how you slip into old patterns of unhealthy thinking. Why do you lose yourself in the unhealthiness of others or why does stress get to you so much? Look at the selection of on-line courses at www.reallifetoolbox.com

c) Choose an accountability partner or someone you can talk to who will keep you motivated to stay on track with the healthy decisions in your life. Accountability partner training courses are available at www.reallife-toolbox.com

d) Choose an accountability system. What do you need to "gate-keep" or what triggers do you need to eliminate from your life so that you stay on track for being healthy?

e) Join an accountability community. Attend a bible study group or join an on-line POD Tutorial group (visit www.reallifetoolbox.com for some options) so that you meet regularly on-line to talk about how to stay on track with healthy and positive thinking so that you can always be in your greatest potential in life by living out God's calling for yourself.

If You Feel Like You Are Sliding

Positive thinking, the motivation to change in healthy ways, and so forth is a regular as well as daily choice. This is part of a process that is not always easy. Often we will slip back into old ways of thinking and the thieves of happiness will rush back into our lives as we become overwhelmed with fear and start losing perspective. We do not "arrive" at being happy or finding inner serenity. Instead, this is part of a process and requires intentional as well as active work each day. Just like with a physical fitness program or regime we maintain our weight as well as health goals, with emotional fitness we need daily healthy habits, resources, and a support system. With fear and negative thinking patterns we lose perspective and forget that we have choices. Our opportunity each day is to **live the choice now** by stepping into healthiness. Now you may feel like the fog of overwhelm will come back into your life or that the negative thinking patterns are beginning to pile up in your mind. Someone may do something or say something that "sends you over the edge" whereby you feel out of control and upset again.

If you decide to "live the choice now", then you will have to actively "unhook" from these people or situations to get yourself back again. In situations whereby you are extremely upset you are giving people the "power to light you up" or throw you off-balance. In many ways you may be like a "Christmas tree" lighting up in reaction to someone else you have given your personal power away to in a negative interaction. Like bulbs on a Christmas tree you are lit up and are powering or fuelling a situation. Unfortunately, being lit up like a Christmas tree in negative situations is not a good thing! In the end you are overcharged and have expended so much emotional energy that you feel burned out.

If you "**live the choice now**", you acknowledge that you are giving other people the "power to light you up." Now you have an opportunity to see what fears are being activated in yourself. This is a challenge for you to grow.

Below are some exercises:

a) Acknowledge you are "lit up."

b) Explore why this person is "getting under your skin", upsetting you, or having the "power to light you up." What fear are they activating within you? How are the thieves of happiness rushing in to take control?

c) Take a piece of paper and draw a line down the center of the page titled healthy (new way) and unhealthy (old way). Write how you could react in an unhealthy way to being "lit up." Then write down how you will react if you are to respond in a healthy way. When you **live the choice now** you have an opportunity to draw a new start line through the center of your life. Furthermore, you have the chance to "step into a healthy response." Each new day there is a new way. You can choose happiness by actively as well as intentionally giving yourself permission to be healthy.

So What Does This All Look Like?

This book has served as an emotional compass pointing you in a particular direction along a journey in which you take negative experiences in life and grow from them as you take a step closer towards your greatest potential as well as God's overall design for your life. While reading this book, we have identified some important milestones or tips for emotional fitness to indicate that you are heading in the right direction. Hopefully you may have even gained some workable tools, skills, or insights along the way to help you in your journey. As many people acquire these skills they want to know what this journey actually looks like in day to day life. Individuals do not "arrive" at healthiness and it is with daily intentional work and thought along with the creation of new habits they start to make significant positive changes in their relationships as well as emotional worlds. So let's look at what this journey is like in one couple's life which we will call Doug and Donna.

Doug and Donna are a couple in their forties with three children who are all in their teens. For years Doug has been struggling with lusting and he is "overly familiar" with the female friends and acquaintances that are part of their life. Doug also has issues with pornography which he "dabbles in" watching from time to time but the source of trust issues really come from his flirtations with other women in front of Donna. As a result, Donna feels humiliated as well as devalued. She is very frustrated with Doug because he tells her that she is overreacting and has a jealous personality. This has been an ongoing issue in the marriage until one day Donna intercepted a very inappropriate e-mail between Doug and another lady in a different part of the United States. They were having cybersex and Doug was describing his sexual fantasy world to this woman on-line via e-mails. Of course Donna was devastated and with all the years of pent up frustration she feels extreme rage which she thinks she cannot express without Doug getting upset so she turns this anger inwards as she manifests these angry feelings into depression. Donna then crashes into bed and has found comfort in food as she "emotionally eats" away her problems. She is rapidly gaining weight and her level of self-loathing is increasing daily. Now with the interception of this e-mail, Donna feels like she is on the verge of a nervous breakdown.

So where do they start?

First of all, Donna can "live the choice now." The emotional boulder in her life is the trust issue with Doug which then results in depression as well as emotional-eating. Donna is beginning to shut-off and shut-down from life which is impacting her relationship with her kids significantly as well. Donna can wait for Doug to make a change but if she waits for him to get healthy and recognize the errors of his ways, then she is handing her serenity to the "If Only Happiness" thief and her life will get better "if only" Doug would stop acting-out. The reality is that if Donna gets healthy herself, then poor treatment from Doug will no longer feel comfortable. If Donna starts to work on her emotional fitness and develop her core confidence then she will start to grow into healthy responses as she raises her value in this relationship. Doug then has a choice to come and "meet her in her value" by addressing his unhealthy behaviours or he will struggle with positive change. This is Doug's choice but what we know for sure is that the dynamics in the relationship will not stay the same if one person starts to grow into healthiness. Relationships are much like a dance and if one partner shifts up the dance steps into healthiness then the other partner has to respond in some way. The old unhealthy dance is no longer at play.

So Donna takes the "one year place challenge" and draws a new start line through the center of her life regardless of what Doug does or does not do. As a result, Donna realizes she has a choice and begins her healing journey. Donna identifies the issue which is one of trust and sees how the thieves of happiness are stealing joy from her life. She begins a process of reclaiming her life back from fear and negativity as she commits to growing as a better person from this negative experience in her life.

Now Donna's emotional world is beginning to open up. As a result of "living the choice now" Donna draws a line between unhealthy and healthy reactions. In an unhealthy way she can continue to eat away her problems and shut-down from life. With a healthy way, she will challenge herself to learn a new toolbox of skills for how to deal with issues in her life as well as her relationship.

Now Donna has options as she can:

-Make a commitment to positive change (CPA). Her commitment is to get herself back because she feels like she is losing herself in Doug's unhealthy acting-out issues. She is going to reclaim her life back from negativity as well as fear.

-Donna can work through the *Core-Confidence: Stepping Into Your Greatest Potential-Stepping Into Your Greatest Life Workbook* as she learns about how to get herself back again and develop the confidence to deal with the issues in her marriage while also finding herself again as she explores who she really is and grows into God's calling for her life. She makes a commitment to becoming healthy within herself rather than rebounding off of Doug's issues or living in the constant oppression as well as fear that Doug is going to "cheat on her" with another woman or that his eyes are wandering elsewhere.

-Donna can take an on-line course and begin creating a toolbox of skills for how to deal with communication and stand up to face the issues in her marriage. There is a selection of courses from www.reallifetoolbox.com that she can choose from as she begins her journey.

For example some on-line courses include:

a) **Core Confidence** (a free four week on-line course to learn how to increase emotional fitness and deal with problems or issues in your life.)

b) **Reclaiming Your Life-** (a forty-eight week on-line program to learn about how to heal yourself from the impact of someone else's acting-out and the resulting trust issues in your relationship)

c) **Boundaries** (an eight week on-line course on how to learn to set healthy limits in relationships)

g) **I Don't Trust You: How To Confront Someone Around Broken Trust And Begin The Healing** (a four week on-line course on how to deal with and talk about an issue of trust in a marriage.) Donna may want to take this course in particular to learn some tools or skills around how to deal with the e-mail issue she found where Doug was sending an inappropriate sexual e-mail to another woman.

d) **How To Communicate With Someone Who Doesn't Communicate** (a four week on-line course around who to deal with a spouse who has issues with communication).

e) **Emotional Eating: Normal, Compulsion or Addiction?** (a four week on-line course to learn about the pattern of emotional eating and how to deal with underlying issues which are driving the over-eating behaviour.) Donna can learn the difference between physical and emotional hunger as she focuses on how to work through her issues of eating away uncomfortable feelings.

-Donna can work out a plan around how she will continue with her positive changes within herself by completing a core confidence or care plan with an on-line wellness coach through www.reallifetoolbox.com

-Donna can keep this commitment to positive action (CPA) going by getting a support system of accountability partners who she checks in with to talk about how she is feeling. If these people wanted training in how to be an accountability partner they could take the accountability partner training on-line course at www.reallifetoolbox.com

-Donna can get together with other women who are dealing with similar struggles and join at POD Tutorial which is like a cyberspace support group and these sessions are led by an on-line wellness coach at www.reallifetoolbox.com

-Donna can do devotionals each day and as part of her prayer time with God she can do a journal entry in her "From Fear To Faith" journal. More details available at www.livethechoicenow.com

Donna is participating in these positive changes within herself and now Doug can join her in this healing journey. Doug has a variety of supports that he can explore as well.

Some options for Doug on-line skills for living classes at www.reallifetoolbox.com which include:

a) **Finding Freedom** (a forty-eight week on-line program for people who are struggling with acting-out behaviours, self-destructive patterns, and/or addictions as they learn about recovery.)

b) **The Road To Healing From Pornography** (a four week on-line program for people who are struggling with pornography and want to begin recovery from these issues.)

c) **Sex: Normal, Compulsion, or Addiction** (a four week on-line program for people wanting to learn about sexual acting-out and sexual addiction as well as how to start recovery on these issues.)

d) **Self-Sabotage: Why When Things Are Going Well Do I Mess Them Up?** (a four week on-line program for people who experience good things happening in life and then manage to sabotage this success by acting-out or self-destructing in ways that cause themselves further problems. In this course participants learn about patterns of self-sabotage and how to change these patterns.)

e) **I Have A Secret: How To Talk About The Trust You Have Broken And Then Begin The Healing** (a four week on-line program for people who have been hiding secrets in their relationships and how to deal with these issues in a positive way rather than living with constant guilt and further deception.)

-Doug may also want to work with an on-line wellness coach on an *accountability and recovery plan* to manage his lusting and sort out how to be healthy in his marriage.

-Doug can join a group of people who are struggling with similar issues through on-line POD Tutorial Support which is like a cyberspace support group and these sessions are led by an on-line wellness coach.

Together Doug and Donna may want to explore couple's supports which include:

a) **New Horizons** (a forty-eight week on-line course for couples wanting to rebuild their relationships after trust has been broken as they begin healing these issues.)

b) **Communication** (an eight week on-line course for couples wanting to work on building healthy communication in their relationships.)

c) **Keeping The Connection** (a four week on-line course for couples wanting to increase intimacy in their relationships.)

d) **Healing Resentments** (a four week on-line course for couples wanting to rebuild trust and overcome resentments in their relationships.)

e) **Healthy Sex and Sexuality For Married Couples** (a four week on-line course for couples wanting to connect in deeper emotional as well as physical intimacy with each other as they learn about how to enhance their sexual health in the relationship.)

-Doug and Donna can also work out a plan around how they will keep going with their positive changes by completing a *Couples North Star plan* with an on-line wellness coach through www.reallifetoolbox.com.

Now Doug and Donna do not have to do everything listed above as they are on a healing journey from their issues. The resources above are part of a smorgasbord of options and ultimately Doug and Donna have to decide for themselves what resources are going to be helpful but if they decide to "live the choice now" they can then open up their emotional worlds and see that there are options as they begin an exciting new healing journey by retiring the old self-destructive patterns of the past.

Live The Choice Now!

One Year Place Challenge

A New Start Line To Healthy!

Each day I make the choice of where to place my mind and my thoughts. I can place my mind into the sea of fear as the waves of stress sweep me into further turmoil. The negativity can consume my soul or I can take a step out of the abyss for even a moment. My choice is to step into the positive. As I draw a new start line to healthy each day I reclaim my life back from negativity as well as fear. I live the choice now as I step out from the shadows and darkness of fear into the light of God's healing. When I embrace this choice my world opens up and I cross the line from "what if fears" to "what could be...potential" as I can now see opportunities as I move from fear into faith. I see what God wants me to see as I embrace my potential, my light, and the Lord's greatest direction. As a result, my world changes because each day I live the choice!

I take the "one year place challenge" knowing that in a year from now as I live the choice each day, I can be in a better as well as stronger emotional place in my life. I live the choice now by making the commitment to be positive and healthy.

References

-Eldredge, John (2010). *Walking With God.* USA: Thomas Nelson

-Frankl, Viktor E. (2006). *Man's Search For Meaning* USA: Beacon Press

-Gerber, Michael E. (1995). *The E-Myth Revisited: Why Most Small Businesses Don't Work And What To Do About It.* USA: Harper Collins

-Nance, Jerry (2009). *From Dream To Reality: Principles For Building A Non-Profit Organization.* USA: Teen Challenge International

-Willard, Dallas (1990). *The Spirit Of The Disciplines: Understanding How God Changes Lives.* USA: Harper Collins

-*All scriptures referenced in *Core Confidence: Stepping Into Your Greatest Potential-Stepping Into Your Greatest Life* are in NIV (New International Version).

Another Book By Cathy Patterson-Sterling...

-I Didn't Mean For This To Happen: How To Repair Your Life And Marriage After Trust Has Been Broken (2012). Available on www.amazon.com

Cathy Patterson-Sterling is an International Christian Author, Speaker, and Registered Clinical Counsellor who has a speciality in helping individuals, couples, and families struggling with confidence/self-esteem issues, addictions, broken trust, pornography, and betrayal. With her experience as a Registered Clinical Counselor and Senior Director for different Drug and Alcohol Treatment Centers for the past fourteen years she has walked alongside thousands of people during their darkest moments in life. Cathy's message is one of hope in that it is within our darkest hours that we find our greatest light.

More Christian couples are having the "I Didn't Mean For This To Happen" conversation which is a crisis in their marriages when one person has broken trust by acting-out with pornography, having inappropriate sexual conversations (sexting), engaging in emotional affairs by having intimate or private talks through texts or e-mail, or with compulsively spending money with online shopping and so on. This crisis of broken trust can be a confusing time and readers will learn why acting-out occurs along with the resulting lies as well as deceptions. Furthermore, readers will explore the steps of the recovery as well as healing journeys involved in repairing their marriages from broken trust.

*Visit www.livethechoicenow.com for more details.

20630697R00095

Made in the USA
Charleston, SC
18 July 2013